Introduction

The articles that are printed in this book made what was in my opinion the most important, the most constructive, series on a single subject that *Good Housekeeping* has published in the quarter century and more that I was its editor. And they might so easily never have been written—just a little item in a newspaper missed, or its significance overlooked, and these sincere and helpful articles would still be locked up in the minds and hearts of the men and women who wrote them. For it all happened just like that. Students in one of the larger California universities asked that a course in marriage relations be given—and a New York newspaper heralded it with a stick of type over about page 10.

Somehow the item impressed me deeply. Here were thousands of students of both sexes, thinking of marriage, physically impelled toward marriage, admitting that they wanted more information about marriage before undertaking it. Add to these students the hundreds of thousands in other colleges and to them the millions of young men and young women outside of college—and there was Youth itself, visioning marriage as the Great Adventure, which no one should miss, but about which there were grave reports.

I have heard lots about Youth in recent years—its lackadaisical attitude toward all serious things, its tendency to look the moral code straight in the eye and smash it, its belief that chastity isn't worth its cost or success in marriage worth working for. And I had disbelieved much that I had heard, it having been my privilege to work with and for young people in high school and college over a long period of years. I knew that Youth is looking for something better than it is being given in either precept or example. And so this request of a group of college young people seemed to me to be both a challenge and an opportunity.

I accepted the challenge. The next step was to find out how best to meet it. It seemed to me that to offer our young people anything less than the best that I could get would be letting them down. So I turned for advice to several college men who had made a long study of the problems involved in marriage, and from the various lists of subjects and authors

3

suggested—adding a few of my own—selected the group now presented in permanent form in this book. If these articles make success in marriage seem something that must constantly be worked for, they at the same time show that success, plus the happiness that goes with it, can be achieved. Which is all, I think, that any man or woman has a right to ask for.

William F. Bigelow

Helen Judy Bond

The Good Housekeeping Marriage Book

Unknown

Foreword

If by some strange chance, not a vestige of us descended to the remote future save a pile of our schoolbooks or some examination papers, we may imagine how puzzled an antiquarian of the period would be on finding in them no indication that the learners were ever likely to be parents. "This must have been the curriculum for their celibates," we may fancy him concluding. "I perceive here an elaborate preparation for many things; especially for reading the books of extinct nations and of coexisting nations (from which, indeed, it seems clear that these people had very little worth reading in their own tongue); but I find no reference whatever to the bringing up of children. They could not have been so absurd as to omit all training for this gravest of responsibilities. Evidently, then, this was the school course of one of their monastic orders."

Herbert Spencer

This quotation from the pen of Herbert Spencer arrested our attention this winter when we were reading a number of books dealing with various epoch-making periods in the development of educational method and theory.

We closed the book and pondered over the inferences made by this leader and we began to speculate on what an antiquarian of the present period might say of our textbooks, our curricula, and our examination papers. We hope in his search that it might be his good fortune to unearth the syllabi of some of our courses on Education for Marriage and Family Life, some of the worthwhile literature which is being written on the subject, even perhaps the *Good Housekeeping Marriage Book*. If these happened to be the only remaining record of the period, we might fancy him concluding, "Ah, what an enlightened people there must have been in the twentieth century. I perceive here preparation for real life problems. This must have been a school course for all the Youth of that generation."

This volume represents a definite step in the advancement of this ideal.

We wish to express to Dr. William F. Bigelow, former Editor of *Good Housekeeping*, our sincere appreciation for the kindly way in which he received the idea of publishing these valuable articles in permanent form and his readiness to help in every way possible in carrying this idea through to completion.

To each author we wish to express our gratitude for the important contribution he has made, not only in giving new interpretation and new meaning to the institution of marriage, but also for rendering valuable assistance in the solution of many of the problems which confront the Youth of today as they approach this most challenging, most demanding, most satisfying and most rewarding of Life's experiences.

H. J. B.

Table of Contents

Chapter

Dr. Ernest R. Groves

CHAPTER ONE

When He Comes A-Courting

Never were American young people more conscious of the challenge of marriage. They are not willing to accept the idea they have often heard expressed by their elders that marriage is a lottery. Neither do they believe that when they marry, they are given a blank check which permits them to draw from the bank of happiness as they please. Instead, even though they do not know how to go about it, they feel more and more that there is something they need to do to give themselves a fair chance of achieving success. A mere acquiescent waiting for Fate to come and lead them into paradise is contrary to their spirit. They seek as best they know how some way of finding their proper mate and some means of becoming equal to the testing that even the most reckless of them in their better moments realize that marriage is sure to bring.

This fact-facing of the marriage problem shows, more fully than anything else could, how much our youth today are expecting from marriage. Even those marriages that peter out and sink to a barren drabness started out with high hopes, and, although the victims may not know what brought about their mishap, they generally feel there was blundering somewhere and that this need not have happened.

Some young people grow cynical because they are so familiar with matrimonial failures; but most of them, even when they have noticed that many of their friends are unhappily married, become more determined to find, if they can, the secret of success. This leads them to ask for help, for insight, and to become fact-seeking with a frankness that seems to be their most marked characteristic. They have not been led into this attitude by any influence from their elders; they have acquired it from their own realistic approach to the marriage problem, which they clearly see has more emotional meaning than anything else that is likely to come to them through choice during their lifetime.

This request for help by young people in courtship, in engagement, in their first years of marriage, and when they plan to assume parenthood, cannot be met merely by words of caution. They do not welcome just being told what they should not do. What they seek is positive assistance. They do not want advice, but they want information and insight. They have become convinced that there are facts about marriage that people have learned through experience, especially through the searching of the scientists, and they ask that they be given the advantage of this knowledge.

These young men and women do not take kindly to a marriage program which merely lists the qualities that one ought to find in one's mate. Even from a very little courtship experience they come to realize that one does not desire to marry abstract virtues, however desirable, but a flesh-and-blood person whom one desperately wants. What they seek is a guidance which will keep them from wanting the kind of person they should not marry. They expect to fall in love, but hope to escape immature, untrustworthy emotions. They want to make a grown-up choice or at least to pick a mate in whose fellowship they can develop the character they know they need to achieve happiness.

First of all they ask for information that will help them make good use of their courtship opportunity. They rightly feel that if they blunder in this period, there is little hope of their making their goal later. They have grown suspicious of a strong feeling of attachment, because they have been forced to see in the experiences of many of their friends that this has not guaranteed later happiness. They expect to have sooner or later an overwhelming impulse to join their life to that of another human being, and they ask:

"How can I protect myself from giving my affection to the wrong person? How can I learn when it is safe to trust my own strong emotions? I know I shall be just as others are, unable to hold back, blind to the other's faults, but surely before this happens I can do something that will keep me from growing fond of a person whom I ought not to marry! People who study marriage and become familiar with its emotional demands must have learned some facts that offer guidance in choosing a life mate."

Indeed, there are such, and here are some that prove useful during courtship, the destiny-deciding period in most people's matrimonial career:

1. Don't let yourself fall in love with the first person who comes along; meet as

10

many young people of the opposite sex as you can.

The young man or young woman should seek to know as many agreeable, companionable persons of the opposite sex as possible without the strain of attempting to establish a reputation for popularity. These acquaintances, as much as possible, should have a background essentially similar to one's own, and they should be sought as friends rather than as lovers. It is obvious that one's affection must turn to some one whom one knows, and before the awakening of strong feeling there should be as wide an experience—the man with women, and the woman with men—as possible. He or she who fails to go about with young people, as opportunity comes, loses the only way there is to gain the knowledge that is necessary later to make a wise choice of husband or wife.

2. Don't judge by party manners and dress; everyday life is different.

In this association with members of the opposite sex, the young man or woman should seek to know, in as many and as everyday situations as possible, those who prove attractive. The party and the dance need not be neglected. Anyone who proves interesting at such occasions must, however, also be known in other more usual and commonplace circumstances. The mere being with members of the opposite sex will not in itself bring insight. One must learn to observe the reactions, the attitudes, the emotional characteristics of anyone whom one likes. Effort must be made to explore the other's personality, not in a cold-blooded, analytical way, but naturally and yet with open eyes, so that there may be genuine understanding of the characteristics of those who seem to be good candidates for matrimony.

3. Study your own emotional reactions as you go along; your mate should bring out the best that is in you.

This association should also help the young man or woman to become better acquainted with himself or herself. Marriage happiness cannot be achieved merely by asking that the other give. There must also be one's own offering in the fellowship. Nothing helps clear up one's own motives, desires, and preferences so much as contact with others. We find ourselves liking some people better than others. We learn to understand ourselves through our own choices. This teaches us that self-acquaintance which measurably helps in choosing the right mate. It is particularly important that we see the effect that others have upon us. What we ourselves possess we are most apt to draw out from others. The kind of mate we need for happiness is one who stirs up the best in us, and not merely the most entertaining or the most physically stimulating of our acquaintances. Matrimony is not a short, hilarious excursion, but a serious lifetime undertaking.

Another thing we want to learn before we choose our mate is the wearing character of any courtship candidate.

4. Does he, or she, wear well? If you are bored now, think of what you may have to endure later.

Wearing qualities are not so easy to find out as some other things; but, if we are alert, we can notice whether a friend who has attracted us holds his own as we go about with him or there is a tendency on our part toward a letting down of interest. Many of those who lose matrimonial zest and merely have a tolerable relationship in marriage blunder at this point. Usually they have not thought of the need of finding out during courtship whether the friendship that started with promise keeps its pace; they have been unconscious of the drift toward a less meaningful relationship, or have assumed that that was an inevitable result of being together constantly. It is true that the emotions do somewhat settle themselves, but they do not become weaker because they are more stable and less violent in expression. Much association with the right sort of person in courtship should increase rather than decrease the emotional ties that hold the two young people together.

5. Will he, or she, grow with you—in mind and in character? If not, your own growth will make you unhappy.

Another of the more difficult tasks that must be assumed in a wise courtship program is discovering whether there are in the person one is beginning to like incentives toward growth. There is one certain thing in any marriage: it is impossible for those who enter such an alliance to remain stationary; either they grow in character or they lose ground. The mere possession of ambition is not evidence of the desire to grow up emotionally.

One has to probe the ideals of the other person. The question is, "Does he or she have the character-vitality to develop emotional maturity?" If this is lacking, successful marriage is seldom achieved, and for one who has gained this trait to be tied to a spouse who cannot attain it is tragic for the well-matured person.

6. Will he, or she, put father or mother ahead of wife or husband? Look out for apron strings.

There is something that the psychiatrist warns us about that we cannot wisely forget in our courtships. We must free ourselves from entanglements in our emotional make-up that may have had their beginning in childhood, and we must especially avoid marrying anyone who has such liabilities and makes no effort to be rid of them. An example is father fixation or mother fixation. We all know from experience persons who cannot grow up from their childhood dependency, and they make very trying husbands or wives. They are easily spotted if one is only keen in noticing what takes place, because they are constantly showing their childishness, and we can be sure that they will continue both to reveal and to nurse their weakness throughout life in such a way as to be discouraging and irritating in marriage and parenthood relationships.

7. Can he, or she, "take it"? You know what they call it in the army.

Although there are many virtues that one would like to find in any candidate for matrimony, there is one that we must look for seriously; if it is absent, turn away from an alliance that is almost certain to fail. That is pluck. Marriage, like life itself, puts upon persons demands that can be met only by courage. The fair-weather type of person is certain to be disappointing in the critical, character-revealing experiences that are bound to arise in marriage and in parenthood. It is difficult not to grow bitter if one finds himself or herself married to a mate who does not have the pluck to meet the disappointments, the hardships, the testing of ideals, that must appear in every husband-wife relationship.

It would be much easier for young people, we often think, if courtship did not make its start at the same time that the young man or woman is feeling in full force the body changes, the nervous readjustments, and the impulses to escape childhood dependency that come with puberty. The fact is, however, that our type of courtship largely results from using the energy of this adolescent upheaval. There is a redirecting of the forces that mark the awakening of puberty and then start flowing through the entire personality. Courtship becomes a sublimation, as the scientist says, a reshaping of this energy so that later there may be a higher, more mature satisfaction of the desires that follow along with this influx of new vitality, this strange, unexpected interest in members of the other sex.

Undoubtedly modern youth face in this experience a greater ordeal than did their parents. This comes about from changes in our way of living and the effect they have had upon marriage, particularly upon our expectations when we enter matrimony. In times past the economic advantages of being married were so great and, as a rule, the struggle of life was so hard, that there was no opportunity to overload marriage with expectations and make its successes and its failures so exclusively the satisfying or denying of emotions.

Of course our tendency is to ask too much of marriage. We demand that it fulfill every purpose of the heart; thus some disappointment, once one enters upon the career of marriage, is inescapable. The young man and woman who have entered marriage expect to grasp much too soon the happiness which their emotions demand. The imagination has such a free range while romance runs at full tide that it would be strange indeed if the imagination did not go far beyond the possibilities of any human relationship.

This readjustment of expectation is what we mean by matrimonial maturity. The young person who refuses to play the game of marriage, just as soon as it appears that complete fulfillment of youthful wishes is not to be had, cannot grow up and never comes to see that the greater satisfactions must come out of self-discipline, emotional restraint, and a love of response that does not ask what is beyond human achievement. Not through a bringing to life of his rosy dreams of contentment, but in a fellowship that deepens through the maturing of emotional life, must one find the values of either marriage or family life.

Although the wise use of courtship is the most important preparation for marriage happiness, it is not the only way we clarify and mature the emotions in our efforts to be happily married. Engagement brings its peculiar

14

challenge, and again demands are made that surge with emotions and need to be dealt with consciously and practically. One of these has to do with sex, and in a very definite way. The modern young man and woman are familiar with the fact that wholesome marriage requires good marital adjustment. They think of this as the sex side of marriage. In recent years they have heard much concerning the need of adequate sex technique in marriage. Not only do they wish information that will prepare them to handle this problem, but often they also need to get rid of their worry that they may fail in this relationship. This anxiety is more common than one might expect, both in men and in women. Even those who are exceedingly sophisticated frequently have such fears. They wonder if they have in some way made their adjustment difficult.

The last days of engagement frequently stir up feelings of doubt. These, born of the thought of the seriousness of the marriage near at hand, easily become allied with the anxious thoughts regarding sex adjustment in marriage. There is every reason for giving young people at this time the information they need to enter marriage as easily and satisfactorily as possible. To give them a fair start we also have to take away the nervous dread that may become their chief difficulty. This must be done not by attempting to extract the emotion as we pull a tooth but by destroying the fear by building up its opposite, security. This is the way we always get rid of hazardous emotions: we destroy them as we alkalize acids.

The reason why so much is made of sex technique as a preparation for marriage is partly that in the past we have utterly neglected this side of marriage and also that it is the easiest problem to handle. Needed information can be clearly and definitely given, and there are a number of excellent books, widely read, that provide this preparation for young people about to be married. Such literature needs to be read calmly so as to avoid exaggeration and not in the spirit of panic that sometimes leaves young people worse off rather than better prepared for their marriage relationships.

Since sex is so highly emotional and its difficulties as they appear in marriage are almost always psychic in character—that is, born of brain experience as a result of earlier suggestions and happenings—it is fortunate that we have something besides a book to offer young people that they may be sure they are well prepared to deal with the sex side of marriage. Doctors

15

have developed a counseling service designed to give young men and young women before they marry the assurance that they need. This is the premarital examination so popular among college people about to be married and becoming more and more a part of their routine of matrimonial preparation.

The young man and young woman, and especially the latter, either together or separately go to a physician who is interested in presenting the sex problems of marriage and is familiar with the technique of the premarital examination and can give young people a clear understanding of the meaning of marital adjustment. This examination includes finding out whether there are any structural or nervous obstacles to marital happiness, the giving of specific information regarding any worry, doubt, or ignorance felt by the person being examined, the giving of counsel that will help make successful adjustment easier to achieve, and, if this is requested, the giving of sound birth-control instruction.

The premarriage examination does so much to lessen the tension before marriage and to prevent temporary discouragements or ungrounded fears after marriage that it is no wonder that it has been accepted rapidly by young people who have come to know its value. Soon it will become a commonplace preparedness sought by all thoughtful, sincere young people who are about to marry. It is best obtained at least two weeks before the wedding. Since there are sometimes mild physical conditions that need treatment and that can be cleared up if there is sufficient time, many doctors prefer that the examination be made at least a month before the marriage. It is true that not every physician is prepared to give this assistance, but the number of those who can is rapidly growing as doctors become conscious of their responsibility for this new type of preparation for marriage.

Generally a most useful part of this service is the opportunity it gives the doctor and the patient to talk together frankly and clearly about sex adjustment so as to take away the emotional handicaps that are the chief cause of maladjustment. These difficulties, when they are deeply rooted, and especially when they are unrecognized, play havoc in marital adjustment. Most often they are the result of some sort of suggestion or happening far back in the earliest days of childhood that led to fear, shame, or guilt, the three chief enemies of happy sex life in marriage.

The mere opportunity to talk over anything related to sex adjustment

16

about which they are anxious brings to many young people a wonderful relief. The best way to get the full value of this service is to read first, as young people are so anxious to do, some sensible, honest, and reliable book that at least in part treats the problems of sex adjustment in marriage, and then to gather up the questions that are personally troublesome or that come because something is not quite clear and take them to the physician at the time of the premarital examination.

Young people should realize also that beyond the value of this examination in itself, it is helpful in that it encourages an intelligent attitude toward all later problems that may arise in marriage. It emphasizes the fact that the best way of dealing with any difficulty is to face it frankly, try to understand it, and then seek the best possible help.

Young people are so conscious of the help they need for the carrying on of their marriage and family career that in every part of the United States we have petitions from students asking college administrators for courses in preparation for marriage. But if every college were giving this instruction, we could not expect that it would reach all American youth. Other institutions and organizations must carry on in the same way, so that other groups than college young people may get their chance to have a modern entrance into marriage. The need of emotional preparedness for marriage must be stressed. The opportunity to start marriage right by bringing the resources of experience and of science should be the birthright of all American youth. These young people seek specific, practical information that will give them insight. They are eager to keep to the pathway leading not only to a satisfying marriage but to a marriage whose meaning goes forward along with our advancing civilization.

Dr. James L. McConaughy

CHAPTER TWO

Now That You Are Engaged

"Love is blind," says the adage. "Love should be open-eyed and wise," say the modern engaged couple.

A successful marriage depends upon two factors—emotions and brains; no marriage succeeds unless these are combined. "Falling in love" is essential, but one can fall out of love as well. Falling in love is the business of the emotions; staying there, holding your lover's affection, requires brains.

A lifetime of happy intimacy between two individuals as different as a young man and a young women can be attained if the mind is used. It is only the old fogy who thinks modern young people "know too much." Psychology teaches us that all emotions deserve study; if they are wisely utilized, happiness results; if they are thoughtlessly spent or thwarted, we may pay the price in unsatisfied lives, broken hopes, sometimes in psychiatric disturbances.

The engagement period—if it is approached intelligently—can be a time not only of supreme happiness, but of wise growth in understanding and preparation for marriage. Unfortunately, modern young people sometimes resent the idea that any one else can help them solve their problems. Advice may seem to them interference. "We are going to live our own lives. Why should any one else care what we do? Why should outsiders feel that they have a right to tell us 'do' or 'don't'?" Such an attitude is understandable, but it is unfortunate, and the young people are the ones who suffer. Perhaps it is true that the older generation feels that it must advise youth, even attempting to control it; but it is also true that we, nearer the end of the road, should be qualified to furnish a map of the way to those about to start out upon it. Thanks to modern scientific methods, the map is now much more accurate than the one handed over to us. There are certain well-charted highroads where there were once only brambled trails.

Among the scientific methods are the statistical studies of marriage; these show certain interesting conclusions. College people have a higher percentage of successful marriages—at least, they show a lower divorce ratio. Apparently college graduates use their minds in picking a mate and in preparing for marriage. Marriages between those who have gone to coeducational colleges appear to have a still higher chance of success. This is probably the result of close association between the sexes in such institutions. But the use of one's mind is what is important; marriage *can* be fully as successful for those who are not college-trained.

According to statistical studies, overdominance by parents decreases the chance of successful marriage. Apron strings never aid engaged couples. A good rule for families is to let the young people avail themselves of parental suggestion, not to force dictates upon them.

Statistically, more marriages succeed if each partner has had an earlier love affair. It is, say the experts, an asset to have had boy or girl friends with whom you thought for a time you were in love. Of course all of us know completely happy marriages of boy and girl sweethearts; most of us also know unhappy couples who first became engaged during their teens, one of whom has entirely outgrown the other, with mismating as a result.

Such mismating is not at first apparent—may not be for several years. The man usually, by the nature of his occupation, meets more people than does the woman. He finds himself in more varied and interesting situations, and may become a more colorful, a bigger person than his wife. Occasionally the converse may be true. At any rate, it is a tragic thing when either husband or wife so far outgrows the other that they have no common interest, no mutual pleasures.

The engagement period is the time to prove the quality of love. Are you—the girl—capable of growth? Can you, harassed by household tasks, keep up with your husband as he develops in the world of men? Are you—the man—so congenial with this girl whom you wish to marry that you will want to share your experiences with her, in situations very different from those of courtship and engagement days?

The engagement period itself is not altogether an easy time. Wise young people can make it one of fuller acquaintance and of growth in thoughtfulness and courtesy. On the other hand, most engaged couples will discover small faults in each other, even when they are deeply in love. Details that had been invisible before may now loom large. Carelessness in personal habits, manners, speech, and attitude may become irritants that jeopardize romance. A trait that may have been a source of amusement before now becomes irritating and exasperating. If the trait is a fundamental one, marriage should be even more searchingly questioned, although the wedding date may be only a few weeks off. Much has been written about the girl who marries a man to reform him; if the reformation is not completed during the engagement, the chances of success after marriage are small.

Yes, this new intimacy of the engagement period may indeed be trying. Tact is required to avoid fault-finding, nagging, and jealousy. A few "lovers' quarrels" do not matter—they give flavor to a romance—but scolding and criticism do. Romance dies when thoughtless quarreling enters. An engaged man should be even more of a gentleman than the courting swain; the girl with a ring on the third finger of her left hand should strive to be even more charming and feminine than the heart-free lass.

Besides the problems of personality adjustment that propinquity presents, there are such questions as these to look into: Is one standard of moral conduct after marriage to apply to both? How free is each partner to be? What opportunity is the girl to have to be herself, have her own interests and friends and money? How soon is the first child wanted? Further—and just as important—the problems of the financial outlook can be worked on during the engagement period.

The wise couple discuss thoroughly their financial setup, draw up a budget, and use their present resources to acquire equipment for the new home. They decide questions which are to form the basis of the marriage and largely influence its success: Is the wife to have her own share of the family income, her own checking account? Must she ask her husband for money for each household expense, or will she have an allowance on which to run the home? In addition, is she to have money for her own personal uses, with no more accounting required than is expected of the husband's expenditures for tobacco and other personal whims?

While such matters are being talked over and decided with mutual consideration, training for marriage itself is under way. The engaged couple may well learn to put into practice two simple yet very helpful suggestions for married people: never both lose your temper at the same time; make the other laugh once daily. They may also acquire an art which contributes

20

definitely to happiness in marriage: playing together.

I think this is sound advice for brides-to-be: If he is a golfer, try to learn enough about the game at least to respond to his enthusiasm. If he fishes, encourage him and try to learn why such a simple sport thrills him. If baseball is his game, do not disdain his choice for an afternoon's relaxation; if he wants you to join him, go and learn enough to enjoy the game with him; if he wants to go with men friends, encourage him, and do not fear this means his love is cooling! (Romance thrives on occasional separations, even occasional vacations from marriage.) Be interested in his doings, but do not be a nuisance.

Grooms-to-be: If she likes bridge, improve your game and avoid embarrassing her by dumb bids and play. If she enjoys art and finds an art exhibit worth while, do not be the dumb male and say that this means nothing to you; let her teach you what pictures can mean—and to real he men, too. If she enjoys good music—going to concerts or listening to the radio—try to share her pleasure and discover what it is that really gives her such satisfaction. In other words, if either has a favorite sport or a hobby, the other should try to join in—at least in the evident satisfaction it gives. Just going to the movies, or sitting on the sidelines watching others play, is not the ideal joint use of leisure; young couples should actually *do* something *together*.

Exercise—active sports—helps keep every one up to par physically; good health is one of the surest foundations for a happy marriage. Divorce thrives among those below par; mental health, serenity, poise, and mutual consideration are all aided by good physical condition.

And remember that mental energy needs an outlet, too. The stimulation of good conversation in mixed groups has a favorable effect on the emotional life of women as well as men. American husbands often err in not drawing out their womenfolk; contempt for their ideas is too frequent.

Those who are wisest about successful marriages advise against long engagements. A hasty marriage and a short engagement are not the same thing. An engaged couple who are sure of their hearts and minds should be helped to marry as soon as the plans for the marriage can be wisely worked out. This usually involves finances—"How soon can we afford it?" Wise parents today cooperate so that the young couple do not have to wait too long. In many cases the older generation, if it can afford it, may give a small allowance to the recently married son or daughter. Money thus given on a definite monthly basis for a previously determined period means much more than a small bequest when the father dies. Or the parents may agree, on a plan carefully thought out, to help if unexpected financial problems beset the young couple. Father may say that if illness overtakes either, or if the first baby arrives earlier than planned, or if a sudden decrease in salary comes, he will gladly help—not with a loan or as a grudging charity but as an interested party to the success of the marriage.

If the man possibly can, he should take out some insurance, seeking unprejudiced advice before choosing between the many kinds of policies each company writes. Even if the policy is small, it is at least a back log if tragedy comes; furthermore, meeting the insurance premiums is a fine first step toward regular saving.

Marrying when either is in debt is to be avoided; such a weight hanging over two young married people all too frequently mars the chances of happiness. And if it is humanly possible, no man should marry while others are dependent upon him.

One comment to engaged students: Unless the circumstances are exceptional, do not marry until your professional training is done. If the girl has her own income or an assured job, perhaps so; if parents will help if an emergency arises, perhaps so; otherwise wait until you are through professional school. Hospitals dislike to appoint married men as internes; they are required to live in the hospital, which means no home life. Law school and marriage do not usually mix well—nor engineering school, nor any other form of post-graduate training. The engaged man who is preparing for college teaching is usually wise if he asks the girl to wait. Many of us know of graduate students who married with only a fellowship or the wages of a wife as income, whose marriages have been almost wrecked by sudden illness or a baby, with resulting financial worries which have aged both the man and woman prematurely. Late marriage for professionally trained men is, apparently, one of the unfortunate results of the long period of preparation for a calling.

The case for postponement is just as strong when one or both are under-graduates in college, with no professional training planned. College

22

marriages are not so wise as marriage after college work is finished. There are exceptions, however; one knows of cases where marriage and return to college to finish was wise. It is unfortunate that some colleges have rules debarring students who marry during the course; secret marriages often result—and these are always to be deplored.

Sometimes parental opposition, or other factors, seem to the young couple to be sufficient justification for a secret marriage. The circumstances which can make this a wise decision are very, very rare. Marriage is a public matter; it should not be hidden. The couple may feel that only their own lives are involved, but they are all too often wrong. Even the best methods of birth control are far from 100 percent dependable; if a baby is coming, the couple face announcements and explanations and recriminations just at a time when serenity and freedom from emotional strain are desirable, particularly for the bride. Secrecy usually means hypocrisy; often it means deceit. Figures show that secret marriages often produce marital unhappiness and an abnormal number of divorces.

The wedding date is chosen by the bride; the honeymoon arrangements are the responsibility of the groom. A wedding is fatiguing, particularly to the girl; the thoughtful man will not plan a long train or motor trip or tiring sightseeing or visits to new relatives; new in-laws can be visited more wisely at a later time. These days should be a period of intimate companionship; a summer camp, perhaps lent by a friend, is ideal. Here, surrounded by nature and not mankind, relaxed honeymooners will find the rest and privacy which should be theirs.

Where to live after the wedding? Obviously where the husband's job is. No need to wait until his chance in the big city comes; the small town is a better place to begin marriage. Friendships come easier, life is simpler and usually cheaper. The divorce rate is much higher in the cities than in small towns or rural regions. Fortunate that couple who start their married life in a town small enough so that neighbors are interested and helpful. The city apartment house is the most impersonal form of dwelling mankind has devised. If the first home does not have all the modern improvements, it is no great tragedy. More marriages are wrecked by too much free time than by too many home tasks to perform. Our grandparents married in the days of covered wagons and sodhouses and drought; a dash of their spirit is a good ingredient in a modern marriage.

Above all else, the engaged couple should plan to have a home of their own, even if it is only two rooms. If economic considerations make them consider moving in with the in-laws, let some one warn them that the adjustment of two personalities which marriage involves demands some privacy beyond that of a bedroom. Parents, no matter how loving and wise, help the newly married most when they do not live under the same roof with them. Loving interference, irritation, nervous tension, usually go with "living with the folks."

If they have to live with the older folks, the young people should arrange to have two or three rooms of their own, with their own privacies, where they can entertain their own friends and be themselves. If they live thus under the parental roof, they can keep their self-respect by paying something a month as rent, no matter how small. Furthermore, they should own their furniture—at least some of it; it should represent their own joint taste; the possession of some lares and penates is a very good basis for a lifetime partnership. The joint possession of material things is almost an essential to successful marriage.

Should the girl hold her job after she marries? Some authorities say that a bride is better off, emotionally more serene, if she has some work—not too fatiguing—outside the home.

Modern young people do not marry until they know that each brings to the marriage bodily fitness. A medical examination, with blood tests, is required in many progressive states before a marriage license can be secured. A doctor's certificate of bodily fitness for marriage is fully as essential as a marriage license. Such an examination gives a feeling of security to each individual and forwards the well being of society.

To many modern engaged couples the most disturbing question is, "Shall we wait until marriage for physical union?" No question, I think, comes up more often in college courses and conferences on engagement and marriage. "We love each other devotedly; why should we wait for a mere license and a public ceremony?" That testimony which trained doctors, sociologists, and psychiatrists give is entirely in favor of postponing all such relations until after the marriage ceremony. Furthermore, statistics show that marriages in which the engaged couple do not "go all the way" seem to have

24

a higher chance of success.

Modern life has made this a keener difficulty for young people than it was for most of us older ones. Inhibitions have largely gone, young people are allowed to work out their own problems; the automobile, tourist cabin, and hotels with careless standards for their guests allow any engaged couple plenty of opportunity, which we largely lacked. If, even though an engaged couple are passionately in love, the temptation does not present itself at all, they are fortunate; there have been millions of happy marriages before in which this has taken care of itself naturally. On the other hand, if they have to face this situation frankly, and decided to wait, they need have no fear that this indicates a lack of sex feeling or that after marriage this relationship may fail because it has not been indulged in earlier.

But let us all realize frankly how often this problem troubles the majority of engaged couples—no matter how fine their principles may be. Understanding and love are more helpful in such situations than general advice and "don't." Assisting the young couple to marry soon is usually the best help we can give.

If an engaged couple are willing to think this matter over as unemotionally as possible, the following points may be considered: Postponement of marriage because of economic conditions has been a problem almost as old as the race; they are not the first couple to face this difficulty. Revolt against the standards of home, church, and society is almost always an expensive decision; secret actions are to be deplored; worry about "what may happen" may destroy the serenity in love which should ideally characterize the engagement period. They should be glad that they do have "sex hunger," but should recognize that each person owes just a little to the preservation of morality and social standards; even if they feel that the conditions which beset them are hard, they should think twice before placing themselves "outside the pale of social sanction."

The engaged young man may well do some special thinking of his own. No birth-control methods are sure; the testimony of medical groups rates various procedures as from 20 percent to 90 percent safe; no man who really loves his fiancée would take the chance of "getting her in trouble." More of the responsibility of this decision rests on the man than on the girl. She may seem to be entirely willing, but the normal girl worries, even if only over what her parents would think if they knew. More than one marriage has been wrecked because of the psychiatric effect upon the girl of such practices during her engagement.

Furthermore, many engaged couples do not finally marry; memories of forbidden intimacies are not going to make it easier for either to give himself or herself fully to the right person later on; premarital relations with another may prove a real handicap to the full realization, later, of an ideal romance and marriage. The complete realization of sex after marriage is never so fully accomplished, emotionally and lovingly, if the two have refused to wait. Even the most sophisticated young people have somewhere inside them hesitations about the wisdom of defying social standards. There is a spiritual side to marriage; practices in secret, unapproved by others, detract definitely from this important phase of marriage.

Even if the young man can convince himself that not waiting is right, in spite of what his fiancée may say, she is unlikely to agree in her heart. Very few men who rationalize themselves into believing that such a course of action is wise would be as willing to have their sister or—some day—their daughter do likewise.

Remember these truths: In married life itself there are many difficult decisions, many things you would like to do, which wisely you do not. You are definitely preparing yourself for marriage in strengthening your character by saying "no" now.

If you have decided not to, do not allow yourselves to be in situations which make it unduly difficult to carry out your decision. Drink stimulates the sex urge; few decent people would enjoy remembering that their first sex experience came when they were stimulated by liquor. If you drink, avoid emotional situations in secret thereafter, until this stimulus has worn off. If you harass your serenity and loving contacts by reopening the decision every time you meet, try to do things together in which this sex element does not present itself as a perpetual problem. One couple beset each time they were together with the difficulty of carrying out their decision not to, deliberately decided to visit art museums together instead of merely "petting"; this new interest minimized the other problem and gave them something most worth while to discuss, and it is now one of the many fine things in their married life.

Margaret Culkin Banning, in *The Reader's Digest* for August, 1937, summarizes "The Case for Chastity." For the engaged couple, the following of her points apply: the girl who is unchaste with her fiancé often hesitates to get competent medical advice; venereal disease is a danger; abortions are dangerous physically and emotionally; fear should never accompany sex; sex experience before marriage may harm sex later on; one's "moral code" is violated; some discoveries should be saved for marriage itself; premarital relations stimulate jealousy after marriage; early marriage is a better solution.

From the sociological standpoint we should take great satisfaction in the increasingly wise way in which young Americans are approaching marriage. Fifteen years ago the subject was entirely neglected in our colleges; today at least 100,000 college boys and girls have the opportunity to enroll in college courses or to attend discussion conferences on marriage. Wise men and women have studied the basis for successful marriage and have written about it. Laws have been changed so that such books—written by American sociologists, doctors, and psychiatrists—are generally available in college libraries today.

However, even the best books do not answer all the normal questions which arise. In many progressive communities marriage clinics have been established, where both engaged and married persons may secure advice from wise, trained authorities.

The ideal consultant is a wise family doctor—especially if he has known both young people from childhood—to whom they can go together for a personal conference. Sometimes the family minister is wise enough to give help.

Appropriate knowledge about sex is necessary for the engaged. Sexual experience is not. Certainly it can now be said—as it could not five years ago—that no modern marriage need be wrecked because the young couple did not know where to turn for helpful advice.

Dr. Ellsworth Huntington

CHAPTER THREE

Ought I To Marry?

"Ought I to marry?" is not a simple question. Its answer is full of a thousand complications. For the great majority of people it is one of the three most important questions that are ever answered or left unanswered in a whole lifetime. The other two are "What is my main purpose in life?" and "What is to be my occupation?" They are old questions, but "Ought I to marry?" is new. In the old days everyone was married as a matter of course. Perhaps in the future the main question will be, "Am I fit to be married?"

"Ought I to marry?" is really three questions in one. First, "Have I a right to marry?" Second, "Is it wise for me to marry?" Third, "Is it my duty to marry?"

You say, perhaps, that these questions are your own business and nobody else's, but you are wrong. They *are* somebody else's business, and the somebodies else are a good deal more numerous than you think. The first somebody is the man or girl whom you want to marry. Will it be good for him or her to marry *you?* The next somebodies are the children whom you and your mate may have. They have a right to be born with a good inheritance, to be reared in good health, and to be well trained in a happy home. Your children's children, too, will have a right to bless you or curse you, according to your way of answering the question, "Ought I to marry?"

But even your children, grandchildren, and great-grandchildren are not all the somebodies who are vitally concerned with your answer. Hundreds of people will be helped or hindered by your home, by the kind of person you become under its influence, and by the kind of children who go out from it. You and "he," or you and "she," are certainly the ones most immediately concerned in the question "Ought I to marry?" but your children's stake in the matter is even greater than yours.

Now for the three questions which are implied when you ask, "Ought I to marry?" First, "Have I a right to marry?" Every young person should ask this question. Fitness includes several aspects, among which the first is physical. The most inexcusable unfitness is venereal disease. There is no meaner crime than for a young man to acquire venereal disease by reason of weakness of will, and then pass it on to an innocent girl and perhaps to unborn children. Physicians say that in spite of so-called modern prophylaxis and supposed cures, syphilis is still alarmingly common, and other venereal diseases are rampant. A person having any of these diseases has absolutely no right to marry. Even if he is pronounced cured, he ought not to marry until a physician pronounces him cured *beyond danger of recurrence*.

For this reason the strictest premarital examination by a competent physician should be required. Marriage should be contracted only after such a physician has given both man and woman a clean bill of health. This is desirable as a means not only of creating a public opinion which will express itself in laws, but of giving both parties a feeling of security. No matter how completely they may trust each other, it is well to have a physician verify the trust.

Another reason for a complete physical examination before marriage is to determine whether it is possible for both parties to have children. Sometimes expert medical advice and treatment make all the difference between a childless home and one that has the happiness of a well-rounded family. In every marriage children should be an essential feature—the most essential feature in the long run. In many countries sterility is sufficient grounds for divorce. In an ideal civilization probably no marriage would be permitted between a person who appears to be sterile and one who appears normal. The sterile would marry the sterile, and the fertile the fertile. Even in our civilization what right has anyone to doom his partner to a childless marriage? The overwhelming majority of people want children. Only the highly exceptional and pitiable woman is without this desire. The normal man feels it almost as strongly as the woman when once the little hand of his own child clasps his finger. Of course unforeseen conditions may unexpectedly make one partner to a marriage sterile, but that is another matter and by no means prevents a happy marriage. In certain cases, too, it may be allowable for a fertile partner to marry one who is known to be sterile. That should never happen, however, without the fullest knowledge on the part of both, and without full time to think the matter over quietly and in complete freedom from the emotional strain caused by the loved one's frequent presence.

Many childless marriages are rendered not only happy but very useful to society by the adoption of children. It should always be remembered that from the standpoint not only of family life but of old age and of society in general, children are the most important result of marriage.

The worst forms of unfitness for marriage are hereditary, but some hereditary defects are mild, some terrible. There is much doubt as to whether many defects are hereditary or are the result of unfavorable conditions during pregnancy and early infancy. Far too much emphasis is placed upon external and easily visible defects in comparison with internal ones which cannot be so readily detected. Such minor hereditary defects as hare lip or misshaped fingers do not necessarily indicate unfitness for marriage. They are far less dangerous than hereditary susceptibility to diseases such as diabetes or weakness of the heart, which lead to unhappy marriages by reason of frequent illness or early death. A hereditary tendency toward short-sightedness or defective teeth, on the contrary, may permit the longest and happiest of marriages. All inherited defects are regrettable, but practically no one is free from them in some minor form.

The sensible attitude toward minor hereditary defects is to balance their real importance against both the good and the bad qualities shown not only by the individual but by his brothers, sisters, parents, and other relatives. Conscientious sufferers from visible defects of any kind are apt to overestimate their importance. Moreover, many supposedly hereditary defects may equally well be the result of an unfavorable environment like that which caused similar defects in the parents. Under ideal conditions they might never appear at all. In such matters, too, the best course is to consult a good physician. Often, perhaps usually, the best thing is merely to avoid marriage with a person showing defects like one's own, and then strive to give your children so good an environment that only the best in them will have a chance to develop. Fortunately the vast majority of people inherit a fairly good assemblage of traits which balance in such a way as to produce normal human beings.

One type of deficiency, however, renders people genuinely unfit for marriage. It takes various forms. One form, easily recognized, is what is commonly called "mental deficiency." By this we mean not merely the kind

30

of mind found in idiots and imbeciles, but that which appears in morons and other "high grade" mental weaklings. Such mental weakness, or feeble-mindedness, is especially dangerous to society because it often afflicts people who are physically strong and attractive, and who are eager to marry. When such persons marry, they exercise little self-control and are likely to have large families. In this respect they are unlike mental defectives of lower types, who rarely have many children and whose children are likely to die young. "High grade" mental defectives tend to marry one another. The result is bad in two ways. First, if the mental deficiency of one or both parents is hereditary, as is often the case, children with defective mental capacity are sure to be born, and will in turn produce other defectives. Second, even if the defects of the parents are due to accident or disease, the children are almost sure to be badly brought up.

The chief type of mental weakness is emotional in nature. Here is a young fellow who as a boy was always a cry-baby and mamma's darling. He is afraid to stand up for himself, afraid of athletics, afraid of girls; and, because of all this, he is lonely, morose, and secretive. Here is a girl of great ability and charm but subject to fits of deep depression. Another young man loses his temper very easily and cherishes resentment for a long time over trivial matters. The girl whom he is interested in is extremely self-conscious and thinks that she is being purposely slighted unless she is the center of everything. Others, both boys and girls, are excessively irritable, very suspicious, inordinately selfish, hysterical, vainglorious, or in other ways show lack of self-control and emotional stability. Later in life such conditions may lead to intense misery. Nevertheless traits of this sort are often combined with very fine qualities in other respects. This renders it extremely hard to decide whether such persons are fit for marriage.

It is extremely difficult to determine whether emotional instability, selfishness, and other undesirable traits are due to heredity or environment. At this point we enter a field of great difficulty because a trait may be inborn, but not hereditary. A child may be born with serious handicaps because some ailment due to unfavorable environment prevented its mother from nourishing it properly before it was born. Such weakness is not truly hereditary. It will not appear in later generations unless the mothers of those generations also suffer from environmental conditions similar to those which prevented the first mother from nourishing her child. It often happens that such conditions are repeated from generation to generation. If this happens very early in the pre-natal life of the child, the results are very likely to be misinterpreted as hereditary.

In the last few decades the study of heredity has been so fascinating and fruitful that biologists have given comparatively little attention to early environmental influences. Recent work, however, suggests that such influences are far from negligible. My own studies of season of birth illustrate the matter. They suggest that the effect of physical environment upon the health of the parents before a child is conceived has an important effect upon the child's future health and achievement.

Only a hint of the chain of evidence leading to this conclusion is here possible. Many investigations of deaths, fatigue, work, and disease, as well as numerous carefully controlled laboratory experiments, indicate that people feel most comfortable and vigorous, and have the best health, when the average temperature for night and day together is about 63°. Nothing is more pleasant than a day of this optimum kind in May or June. At midday the thermometer rises to 70° more or less; at night it falls low enough so that people sleep soundly and restfully.

A study of season of birth in many countries indicates that children who are conceived when optimum weather of this kind arrives in the spring have stronger constitutions and greater powers of application than do those conceived at any other season. Evidence of constitutional vigor is found in length of life. In four large groups of Americans and in one of Italians it has been found that those born in March, and therefore conceived in June at the time of optimum weather, live longer than those born at other seasons. Among 39,000 people who were born in the eastern United States and who lived beyond the age of two years I found that on an average those born in March lived 3.8 years longer than those born from July to September.

Other evidence, into which we cannot go, suggests that man, like other animals, inherits a definite seasonal cycle of reproduction. As the temperature rises toward the optimum in the spring the functions of the body change in such a way that not only is there a pronounced feeling of well-being, but the children conceived at that time have more than the average vigor, and hence correspondingly long life.

32

The evidence that these children have greater powers of application, or at least that some of them do, lies in the birthdays of eminent people in countries as diverse as India, Spain, Russia, England, France, Germany, Sweden, and the United States. In all these countries the percentage of eminent people conceived when the optimum weather prevails rises much higher than does the corresponding percentage among ordinary people. Moreover, the greater the degree of eminence, the more marked is the contrast with people as a whole.

The reason for this condition must be that the vigor which gives to many people long life gives to highly gifted people a sort of power of steady application and hard work—an emotional stability—which enables them to use their faculties to the best advantage. Thus they achieve fame in greater measure than do equally well-endowed persons with less vigor. There is not the slightest reason to suppose that children conceived at one season of the year inherit any better minds than do their brothers and sisters conceived at other seasons. There is equally little reason to believe that the average inheritance of mental ability declines as the period of conception approaches midwinter, the low point in the seasonal cycle of reproduction. On the other hand, length of life furnishes evidence that physical vigor varies according to the degree to which the mothers at least, at the time of a child's conception, have been under the influence of environmental conditions which assist the germ cells in developing into vigorous babies. Many studies of eminent people show that they are uncommonly long-lived. When deaths in war and by accident are omitted, the average length of life of 11,000 people in the British *Dictionary of National Biography* was 71 years. Eminence and the kind of constitutional vigor that leads to long life go together.

This brings us back to the problem of fitness for marriage. If the effect of the weather on the vigor of parents can have such an influence on health, longevity and achievement, such conditions as diet and mode of life may produce similar effects. This possibility adds still greater interest to the two-edged bearing of what we have just been saying upon the problem of fitness for marriage. In the first place it appears that an unexpected number of weaknesses which are sometimes considered hereditary are environmental. Nevertheless, they are also inborn and cannot easily be eradicated by education. Therefore the chance that ordinary normal people carry a dangerous heredity is reduced, but the responsibility of parents to see that their children are properly born is increased. In the second place, it becomes more evident than ever that fitness for marriage implies intelligent willingness and persistence in acting upon the discoveries of science in whatever way may be best for the unborn child. We have long insisted upon the right environment for the expectant mother during pregnancy. The new discoveries suggest that we must insist equally upon the right environment and manner of life before pregnancy begins.

This brings up a very interesting question upon which biologists are not agreed. Does what has just been said about the period before pregnancy apply to the father as well as the mother? Many biologists doubt whether we have any proof that environmental influence can weaken the sperm cells of the male in such a way that the offspring are thereby weakened. Other biologists, such as Professor Pearl, of Johns Hopkins University, and Professor C. A. Mills, of Cincinnati, have made some interesting experiments which lead them to believe that sperm cells weakened by environmental conditions may affect the vitality of the developing offspring. In short, at the present time there is no agreement among competent scientific men that the health and mode of life of the father, as well as of the mother, influence the physical well-being of the developing child, and thereby affect its emotional stability and other qualities. Until this question is scientifically settled it is obvious that the men best fitted for marriage and parenthood are those who act in such a way that they cannot harm their children no matter which view is correct.

Let us return once more to the problem of deciding how far the mental and social characteristics of ourselves and of the persons we are interested in are due to inheritance and how far to pre-natal and postnatal environment. In the present state of knowledge no exact decision is possible. Nevertheless, in some families an undesirable trait is exhibited by a parent, brothers or sisters, and perhaps by more distant relatives. In such cases, it is probably inherited, or at least due to an inherited deficiency or tendency of some sort, and there is a chance that it may be handed down to the next generation. On the other hand, many persons who suffer from some form of emotional instability come from families in which the parents and near relatives appear normal in this respect. In such cases it is probable that the

34

trait is not hereditary, but due to some influence in pre-natal life or childhood. Until the sciences of human genetics and eugenics have made more progress, the safest way to judge in such matters is by the qualities of a family as a whole.

Whether you have any doubt about this or not, a thorough examination by a good physician who is also a psychiatrist and a man of fine character will be a great help. The physician must frame his judgments for the good not only of the individual who consults him, but of the prospective partner, and of the children who may be born to such a couple. Even the best physician is often unable to decide whether a given defect is hereditary. He can merely frame an opinion based on the *whole family*. Young people find it hard to believe that they marry into families, but they do. As the old Jewish saying puts it, "It is not good to marry a maid who is the only good maid in her family." The responsibility that thus rests on physicians is tremendous. That of the young people who wish to be married is also great, but very different. Theirs is to submit themselves fully and frankly to the physician's examination and advice. He may decide that it is safe to marry a person of stable temperament, but not one who is nervously unstable.

It must always be remembered that even if the physician has given you a clean bill of health, you are still unfit for marriage unless you are willing to go more than halfway in adjusting your life to "his" or "hers." Lovers generally feel sure that they can do this, but have you proved it in your treatment of parents, brothers, sisters, and friends? If you are free from transmissible disease and innate defects, and if you are capable of having children, it is still unwise for you to marry unless you display good evidence of the qualities which make a happy home and insure the right training of children. Darwin once said that the trouble with mankind is not lack of ability, but failure to use the abilities that we possess. Even if it is not wise for you to marry now, perhaps you can take yourself by the scruff of the neck and make yourself fit.

If you are fit, the next question is, "Is it wise for me to marry?" For the vast majority of people the answer is emphatically "Yes" both for your own sake and that of society as a whole. For most people the married state is happier and more useful than the unmarried state. Biologically the two sexes are meant to live together. Long experience has proved that the only

35

permanently happy way of living together is as husband and wife. If the marriage is of the right kind, both the man and the woman become happier, healthier, more adaptable, more interested in the community, and, in many cases, better workers. Marriage is unquestionably one of the best schools and one of the best health resorts. It often has a wonderful effect in steadying people's nerves, provided the partner is wise as well as loving.

The probability that any given marriage is wise is greatly increased where the two young people have reasonably similar ideals and habits and are sufficiently intelligent so that each can enjoy the interests of the other. It is increased still more when both the man and the woman realize that marriage is a comparatively hollow affair unless entered into with the purpose of having a family. Few experiences have greater value than the sacrifices which parents must make if they are to create a real home. The making of such a home brings out the best that is in people. Hence from the purely personal standpoint marriage is a priceless advantage.

There is a social as well as a personal side to marriage. The unstable conditions of the present century have made some people believe that the family is a thing of the past, but this is a mistake. The family life of the future will be different from that of the past, but the finest traits in it will still be the same. Loyalty of each to all and all to each is one of the greatest assets in this tumultuous, changing world. In times of distress, whether it is financial or mental, the most pitiable person is the one without family ties. A family of children may be a handicap at such times, but often it is the very thing that keeps people from failure. Moreover, in adversity and old age a family group of loyal brothers and sisters, even if each has several children, gets along much better than does the man or woman who fends only for himself. It pays to be married and to be married into a large family.

Let us turn back again to the question of whether family life is going to die out. In the old days of unrestricted families children just came because it couldn't be helped. Today, regardless of race or religion, intelligent people limit their families. Abundant statistics make it clear that the size of families has dropped greatly among all except two groups. One is a large group of less intelligent, isolated, shiftless, or incompetent people, among whom families of eight to fifteen children may still be found. The other is a small group of intelligent, high-minded, well-established, well-to-do families with many relatives and with a very assured position. Their children usually number from four to eight. Most of us belong to a huge intervening group in which the average number of children, including those who die young, is less than three, instead of seven, as was the case a century or two ago. This great middle group is the one that will determine what kind of people live in this country in the future.

Well, then, from what part of this middle group will most of the children of the future be derived? A little arithmetic will help us. Suppose we have two sets of parents, numbering a thousand each and having children old enough to be married. In one set each pair of parents has two children; in the other five. The children of each set behave like their parents in this respect. In both sets 15 percent of the children die before reaching the age of marriage, and 10 percent of those who grow up fail to marry. These are normal percentages. Among those who marry, however, 20 percent of the two-child group, and only 10 percent of the other set, fail to have children. How many parents will there be in each group at the end of three generations? If we make no allowance for the fact that more boys than girls are born, there would be 136 parents in the two-child group a century hence, and they would have 136 children. On the other hand, there would be 8744 parents and 21,860 children in the five-child group. Over a hundred and sixty times as many!

Now that we have done the arithmetic, what does it mean? Of course in actual life the two-child and the five-child groups will intermarry. And even if each marries its own kind, the number of children will fluctuate. Nevertheless, there is plenty of evidence of three great tendencies. First, certain kinds of families tend to be small or large as the case may be. Second, each kind tends to marry into its own kind more often than into the other. And finally, people who grew up in large families generally like large families and want to have them. Hence the result of the present limitation of families must be to make large families and family life in general more popular in the future than at present.

This is the way it works in the great middle group to which most of us belong. Families of four to six children are found mainly among people who love children and are willing to make sacrifices in order to provide homes for them. So as long as our present limitation of families continues, the children of each successive generation will tend in larger and larger numbers to be the descendants of people who believe in family life and are willing to make sacrifices for it. A few of them are disappointed because their children do not turn out well, but the great majority feel well rewarded. Ask parents of three or more children how they feel about it. Nine out of ten will say that nothing in their lives has been worth more than their children. So long as people of that kind have children, and those of the other kind fail to have children, family life will not die out. It will become more and more the great center of society. It will change, but the change will be growth, not decay.

Now for the third question, "Is it my duty to marry?" Future generations may say that the better your physique, the greater your beauty and strength, the finer your mind, the more lovable your temperament, and the more highly you are endowed by nature and training, the more certainly it is your duty to marry and have a family. At present, however, the answer to "Is it my duty to marry?" is very much like the answer to a question which you might ask if you were a guest at a delightful summer resort. "Is it my duty to go swimming, play tennis, go yachting, and have a good time?" Assuming that you are physically fit, it certainly is your duty if your presence will cause your hosts and the rest to enjoy themselves. But why ask such a silly question? You will do all those things just because you want to. You would be an awful fool to pass up the chance of having all sorts of fun when everything is just right for it. And you would be an awful fool to give up marriage if the conditions for that were equally favorable.

Of course there is a very important personal element in all this. Some minor crudity in him or her, some ideal diverse from yours, some unfortunate habit or tendency, may be more than you can adjust yourself to. You alone can decide that. All that we can do here is point out what the marriages and families of thoughtful, conscientious people mean to the world.

The essence of the whole matter, as has been said a thousand times, is the extremely rapid fall of the birthrate, especially among intelligent, farsighted, industrious, progressive people whose ideals of family life are high. The majority of the young people who read this article probably belong to this class. Therefore you represent a type of family whose loss or diminution is a very serious matter. Unless your type of family averages more

38

than three children, the country suffers two great losses. It suffers these losses because under the present conditions it takes more than three children per family on an average to provide two who become parents and thus replace their father and mother. So unless your grandparents have at least ten grandchildren, your family stock is dying out, and the country is suffering two great losses. One loss is your good biological inheritance. This does not mean that you are anything wonderful. It simply means that you belong to a group which on the whole inherits more than the average capacity. Therefore, unless you have more than three children, the biological inheritance of America will be lowered.

The second great loss is cultural. It is all very well to talk about sending every competent boy and girl to college, and giving every one the fullest chance to develop, but this does not solve the problem. No other institution comes anywhere near the home as a place in which to establish the ideals and habits that determine whether our lives shall be a mere flash in the pan or a fire that warms and cheers. The finer things of life wither and die if there are not enough children in the families of people who know how to make real *homes*. If you came from such a home, and especially if your relatives also have such homes, you can make one yourself. Few things are more needed in America today than just such homes.

Ought I to marry? I wish that every reader could answer in the affirmative.

Eleanor Roosevelt

CHAPTER FOUR

Should Wives Work?

Is it possible for a woman to marry and still have a career? This question has been asked of me so many times that I am glad at last to sit down and write some of the things which always come to my mind.

To begin with, the question is foolishly worded, for there are very few women who have careers. Those with real careers are a little group by themselves needing separate consideration. Most women marry and work, and the work will not be a "career." The question put this way also seems to imply that marriage in itself is not a career. Anyone who believes that has no real understanding of marriage.

There is no general answer which any one individual can give to this question, no matter how it is worded, for it is one of those questions that depends for its answer largely upon the individuals involved, both men and women.

The question should really be phrased in this way: Are you able to carry on two full-time jobs? Have you the physical strength and the mental vigor to do this day in and day out—particularly when you are young, first married, adjusting yourself to a stranger's personality, and perhaps bearing children, which is an added physical strain?

I can hear you ask, "Why do you say, 'adjusting yourself to a stranger's personality'?" The answer is quite simple: no two people really know each other until they have been married for some time, and one of the most exacting duties of family life is the adjustment of the various personalities that make up the family circle. The mother adjusts herself not only to her husband, but to each of her children and to the other near relatives, and she tries to explain and to adjust them to one another. It is not always an easy task.

More and more households are being managed by the housewife alone, particularly among the young people. That means pretty nearly constant attention to household tasks, if a good job is to be done, in the same way that it would be done in an office or wherever the woman might be0 employed for pay. This housekeeping job can be as scientific and as engrossing as any office job, or it may be a slipshod, haphazard affair with everything at sixes and sevens. It all depends upon the woman whether she makes this side of marriage a career or not.

There is another important aspect to this career. Any woman who means to make marriage a successful career will study her husband, his capabilities, his interests, even his peculiarities. She should know about his business and about his pleasures. It is possible for her to be a great factor in his success, not by thrusting herself forward as an advisor, but by understanding so well his character and his career that she can supplement his shortcomings, bring out the best that is in him, and expand his interests by adding her own. Thus she can have a vicarious career by virtue of what she has put into her husband's.

Perhaps the woman who does this is the happiest and most successful woman, but she has to have the kind of temperament that can do it and do it well, and in addition the circumstances of married life have to make it possible. We might as well face the fact that today circumstances are making it more and more difficult for a woman to lead what two generations ago was considered the normal and natural life for any woman. In those days even a woman who did not marry tried to find a niche that she could fill in somebody's home. A maiden aunt or cousin often took the place of a nurse or governess or even a hired servant and was looked upon with pity, and expected to work early and late for her room and board, and to be as devoted to the children of the family as though they were her own.

Women today would not accept this situation so calmly, and the fact that they can be and are largely self-supporting changes their economic condition. It also changes their relationship to men and marriage.

The economic situation is such today that few young people can marry at the age when their grandparents did. Many young people, rather than put off their marriage indefinitely, get married with the realization that both of them will have to continue working and that children are out of the question until they have laid enough money aside or the man has had enough increase in salary to take care of all the family expenses.

This is not a case of whether you prefer marriage or a career. It is a case of marriage and work together, or no marriage and work alone. Work must go on in either case. For most women there is something so satisfying in creating a home that they do it frequently by themselves. It seems to fulfill a deep inner need to do the little homely things of everyday living, and I think that is one reason why so many young people get married and set up homes of their own long before their financial resources warrant it.

If they want to have children as soon as they are financially established, they usually do so, but a craving for a home of her own is the first stirring of maturity in a woman. To many women, however, a home is not wholly satisfying unless she is making it for someone else, and nature has made most women yearn for a man to mother.

I know one young couple who were married when the boy was getting twenty-five dollars a week and the girl was getting the same as a stenographer. Both of them went on working. Everything seemed to be going very well, and she managed her two jobs quite successfully. The most successful part of it was the fact that she induced her husband to feel an equal responsibility for the house. I remember that when I dined with them, he put on an apron after dinner and helped wash the dishes as naturally as if that were the normal occupation for a man. When a marriage works out this way, it is very successful, especially if the man has a knack for doing things about the house, because it keeps him busy when his wife is busy.

Children can be postponed if two young people have a home and a mate. If a woman has to work to have a home and husband, she will do it happily, but I do not think that always means that she longs to work. It is unfortunate that so often she is forced to for material security.

Where circumstances verge on poverty, marriage is even more of a career, for then more depends on the woman's ability to manage. Of course, when it comes to the mothers of families who work in mills, factories, and stores, we know quite well that there is no question of choice—poverty drives them, and they work because they have to, and only a few would hesitate if they were offered an opportunity to stay at home and look after their home and their children.

I remember visiting a mill town once, and as the women came off the night shift—for there were no laws at that time in that particular state against women's working on night shifts—they met their husbands going to work on the day shift. We followed one woman home. Tired from the hours in the mill, she nevertheless had to set to work immediately to get the children fed and off to school. Then she had her house to set to rights, washing and ironing to do, and dinner to get for the children and supper to be left for the man when he came back from work as she went on. In the afternoon she snatched a few hours of sleep, and the children who were not in school played unwatched and uncared for. She knew that her home life was not satisfactory, and she did not work long hours in the mill because she wanted to, but simply because there was not enough food to go around unless her earnings supplemented those of her husband.

There are women, however, who work for the love of working. They may love their homes and their children and still crave the satisfaction of doing a job themselves. Sometimes it is just because they love the kind of work they do; sometimes it is because they must have the independence which being able to earn money gives them.

I know one young woman who has managed to develop for herself work which she can do in her own home. She feels that her children need her at home, and yet she was very unhappy without some outside interests. She had a musical talent which she shared with her husband, and together they developed a unique project which involved research and execution, giving them a joint interest and allowing her to earn a little extra money.

Very occasionally it is possible for a man and a woman to work together and to have an even closer tie than they would have if the woman remained the man's helpmate only in the home.

The happiness of husband and wife is often wrecked by too little dependence on each other, for to be happy two people must need each other in everything they do. I could tell you many stories of young people who have drifted apart partly because the man was too absorbed by his business and the woman did not have enough to do. One story I remember, however, is a little different, because it was a case in which both the man and his wife had interests which were so divergent that neither of them took any pleasure in being with the other or in hearing about what the other was doing. The man wanted to lead a rather quiet life, and the woman was young and pretty, active-minded, physically energetic. She wanted to do something which would bring in money and make it possible for her to have some of the luxuries and pleasures that she coveted and to which her husband was completely indifferent. They stuck to their own interests, and while they lived in the same house and while they had children and while they were never separated in a formal way, they could not have been further apart if they had lived at the two poles. I question if the children ever knew what it was to feel a community of interests in that home.

It would be well if men realized the need that some women have for a little financial independence. Occasionally marriage is wrecked because the woman feels that her work at home is as much a financial contribution as is the man's work out in the world. She finds no recognition of this in their relationship or in their environment and becomes more and more restless and dissatisfied.

I remember one woman saying rather bitterly to me once that she made more money by saving and good management than her husband did, but that he seemed to think the generosity of giving was all on his side, forgetting that she gave her strength and her time. The work which she did she might have paid someone else to do; and her careful buying actually put in the bank money which her husband could use in his business.

As a rule, the woman spends the major part of the family income, but if it is given her for the house and she has to resort to subterfuge to get any personal pocket money out of it, it is not a happy arrangement. Of course, when two people are planning together every penny of expenditure, the case is different; but when a man has any money which he calls his own, a woman should have some also in recognition of the services she performs for the home. She is more apt to make her housekeeping a good job and to be happy in her family relations.

In many cases a woman who holds a job feels that she is a better companion for her husband because she has more individuality and comes to him more full of different interests when they meet. She may not have the kind of temperament which makes it possible for her to bring up her children herself. She may find that even with less time to give them, she can really do more for them. All these things are subjects for the individuals to consider and decide together.

"Why do you work?" I once asked a friend of mine who seemed very weary.

She smiled and said: "I work because I found that when Stephen came home at night, I had nothing to talk to him about. He is out in the world and meets people and does things. I was in a little backwater and lost the habit of thinking about the same things that are on his mind. I had to go back to work to regain the same atmosphere and to be a companion."

"But," I said, "you have to pay some one to take care of the children. "Wouldn't it be cheaper to do it yourself?"

"Far cheaper," she said, "but even the children are better off. Now, when I come home, I am full of interests I can share with them, and I am nowhere nearly so impatient as I used to be when I answered their questions all day long and directed every minute of their lives. I do not mind now saying, 'Johnny, wash your hands,' or, 'Sara, don't bite when you fight.' I have to do it only between 6 and 8 p.m. But if I do it from 6 a.m. until 8 p.m., many a harsh word is spoken, and many a hasty gesture passes between us, much to my regret afterward."

One thing is certain: Any woman who decides to work after she is married must have good health and be a fairly well-disciplined person, and her life must be systematized so that one part does not interfere with the other, and the man must understand and sympathize with her interests and desires.

The man's temperament is as important as the woman's, for there are men who deeply resent their wives' doing any work and who want to feel that their home is entirely dependent on their own efforts. There are other men who go even beyond that and want to feel that the woman whom they have married is dependent upon them for all she has in a material way, forgetting often that their mental and spiritual contacts count also in any relationship. Then again there are men who, if their wives are self-sufficient and capable, will do exactly what so many women are accused of doing—become parasites and willingly allow themselves to be taken care of in every way, even in a material way.

I knew one man whose wife mothered him until he completely lost his initiative. He was sweet to her, but he really felt that life was made by her and he had to make no effort. Suddenly he met a woman who was weaker and more clinging than he was, and she awakened in him all his dormant chivalrous instincts. He asked his wife for a divorce. He married the weaker woman and became a strong man. The first wife remade her life, which was not astonishing; but he remade his, which seemed unbelievable.

All the things I have mentioned and one more enter into this question of whether a woman who has the ability to do a job outside the home should do it or not. In the last few years I have been getting many letters from women whose husbands have fallen ill or died and left them alone or with dependents. Those who have had no training are the most pathetic, but those who once worked and then gave up altogether are in almost as difficult a position.

I doubt that it is ever wise for a woman who has once had a skill to allow herself to lose it entirely, for, granting that she makes of marriage a career, there may come a time when she will need work, and there will certainly come a time when her children are grown. If the demands on her time are fewer and she is well, she may feel the necessity of taking up some kind of regular work again, particularly if in her youth she was trained to keep busy. This may not be a financial necessity, but merely something to take the place of the duties which were hers when marriage was her only job.

In my own experience I have found there is one other thing that may happen to a woman. For some reason she may have to interest herself in things that have seemed to be more directly her husband's interests and in which she never expected to take any personal part. She may find she becomes interested for a variety of reasons. This necessity of developing interests of her own which take her out of her home will find her better equipped if she has once done a job for pay and kept on doing it now and then throughout her life so that she is able to maintain a professional attitude toward all work, both in her home and out of it.

There are just a few women who have special gifts, who have established careers before they meet the men they wish to marry. If they give up these careers, they may find much of the savor of life is removed when they are not doing something which requires independent thought and initiative. These are the women who go to work because they are conscious of a capacity within themselves which cannot be denied, and they should marry only men who understand this and are willing to make some compromises. It can be done very happily, but it depends on both the man and the woman in each case. These "career" women do a job for the love of

46

it. They may be so gifted that they can cope successfully with household affairs from the administrative point of view. They may not be interested in doing any of the homely things of life. They may be quite helpless at home and need someone else to cope with household measures. For them it is probably impossible to settle down to a homemaker's career and watch over somebody else's career and development and achievement. They are fortunate if they marry the right men!

The women who I feel should undoubtedly have outside occupation, however, are the women whose homes are taken care of by competent hands and feet other than their own, who with ordinary capacity for management can give the necessary orders in fifteen minutes every morning and have the rest of the day in which to do nothing. These women might as well do something even if they have no special gifts, for as idlers they encumber the earth. They are not doing things at home that keep women busy and happy.

I think any young couple is fortunate when the woman has to do everything about the house and does it happily, but in view of all the different angles that this problem presents, I would give no advice, only urge young people to think over what they want out of life very carefully when they are making the decision of how they will start their life together.

Gladys Hoagland Groves

CHAPTER FIVE

Learning to Live Together

The wedding shuts one gate and opens another. The longings and dreamings of courtship are at an end. The supreme intimacy of life begins.

As John and Mary move away from the altar, pronounced man and wife, they know they are starting a great adventure. His beaming face masks a stiff determination to keep his bride happy in spite of any worldly obstacles. Her radiance hides a solemn inward vow to do everything humanly possible to make smooth the way of their life together. They are right. Unless they are very different from most people, this new joint enterprise is going to mean more to each of them than anything else ever can.

Before them is a clear road. Not to happiness, as they may believe, but to the opportunity for gaining happiness. The goal is not easily won, but they can attain it without the aid of luck or rare gifts or miracles—simply by practicing the common everyday virtues that bring success in all human ventures.

A young couple's engagement period is like any other time of excited anticipation, when one has received the promise of something greatly desired, but must wait awhile before its delivery. The happiness of the waiting period is characterized by the absence of a critical spirit, and therefore is apt to be thought of as an experience of pure delight. But the first days of marriage bring out a different set of feelings—those that come when one has definitely obtained possession of anything that before was only promised. At first the emotions seem to stand still—this is the long-coveted moment! Then one begins to appraise. Is the object of one's wishes as desirable as one had expected?

Because reality rarely measures up to imagination, the first answer is almost bound to be, "No, this is not what I expected." And the first emotion tends to be disappointment. If one accepts the fact that discrepancy between imagination and reality is inevitable, he is better able to go on to a more thorough examination of the situation, from the fresh viewpoint of finding out just what he has received, regardless of hazy but optimistic expectations; and the object possessed will more than likely turn out to be better than, although different from, what the imagination pictured.

Knowing that a fleeting sense of disappointment is not peculiar to one's own marriage, but likely to occur in all, as in every other human undertaking, takes away its power to hurt. Unworried by any fear of calamity, each marriage partner can turn to account his or her powers of discernment by learning to recognize the assets as well as the liabilities of the partnership.

Roughly, both the helps and the hindrances to married happiness can be lumped under one word—personalities. Temperament, mannerisms, tastes—all that is implied in the distinct individuality of each person—make up the chief source of the advantages and disadvantages with which the couple enter marriage. These traits cannot be changed overnight. Nor is it necessary, or at all wise, that they should be. John attracts Mary, and she appeals to him, because the personality of each one is what it is. Love has grown up between the two as a result of this personality attraction. And love is the motive that will make both try to keep open the pathway to marriage success.

But love is not a finished product that, once it comes, can forever after be trusted to keep its strength. Like everything else that is alive, it must be kept growing through exercise, or it wastes away.

Love gives the push that keeps a marriage moving, but it does not give the direction. That comes from understanding and cooperation. Although John and Mary love each other as feverishly as any other couple at first, if their loved is self-centered and ingrown, it will eventually turn to hate, or wear thin and give way to indifference. This is what they must guard against. While love is still the moving force of their lives, they must study the problems that are due to come. To wait until they are beset by them is to beg for trouble.

In order to cope with their problems they must realize, first, that they cannot stumble upon married happiness; that they must possess and cultivate a positive will to succeed. Then they must understand that the will is in itself not enough; it must be coupled with a willingness to work, and work hard, for the happiness that can be the greatest blessing of their lives. And finally, they must know what constitutes a happy marriage—what to aim for in their day-to-day association.

What makes a successful marriage? Here are nine guideposts to help John and Mary along their road:

1. The first requirement is the building of a union that is just to both.

The smaller issues on which this rests are the lively clashes of opposite desires, inevitable in the coming together of any two persons, intensified when those two persons are as different as a man and a woman, and unavoidable for two committed to a lifetime together in the close quarters of marriage.

2. Compromise will lift these essentially petty decisions of precedence above the level of selfishness.

Decisions must be made on the basis of what is good for both, not the selfish or narrow wish of either. The choice that brings the larger advantage to the two persons in their common role of marriage partners is the one to be made. Human judgment being as faulty as it is, time may show that any one decision has been an error, but there can be no ill will about it if each feels that an honest effort was made to be fair.

For example, Mary wants to buy a car, just as John is reckoning that the time has come to build a house. Or perhaps he wants to invest money in professional or business advancement at the precise moment when she realizes she wants a child. In either situation, the particular couple involved have to weigh delicately the effect on their joint enterprise of the conflicting courses of action. Much as Mary may crave a child or a car, she might not be able to enjoy either if she got it, unless John were ready to share in her delight. Nor could he, overruling her against her will, find in his choice of home-owning or personal-career investment the satisfaction he had expected. They two, and nobody else, can make the decision to fit their marriage.

Readiness to try to imagine the partner's point of view has to be supplemented by calmness in considering the probable effect of either course on both persons. If each one is hurt at the other's inability to join instantly in his, or her, plans, they will need to take pains not to get sidetracked into making a personal contest of the affair. Trying to win over your partner with a single eye to getting what you want, regardless of its effect on the mate, is short-sighted in the extreme. Even if you could care only for personal pleasure, that cannot long outlast your spouse's displeasure.

Staging a contest or a succession of small contests, for the sake of finding out who is boss builds up a habit of fighting that may lead to a bitter end. It is useless to discover who can win in any particular skirmish. What is important is to learn whether one of you is set on being "head of the house." If your spouse craves that distinction, by all means hand it over without delay. It is an empty honor, for the one who bends but does not break will readily develop the fine art of influencing the headstrong one.

Because it is part of the traditional feminine character to enjoy giving in to the man, this tendency must be scrutinized when it appears. No man can afford to be crippled for life by letting his wife swaddle him with solicitude as some mothers spoil their children for their own glorification. A woman's feeling that she will be emotionally gratified by making a sacrifice does not prove that, aside from her momentary pleasure, there is any value in it. The ease or difficulty with which husband or wife makes an adjustment in no way measures the worth of that adjustment for their partnership.

Because of women's recent growth in socially recognized independence, any individual woman may waver between a craving for self-sacrifice and a repugnance to the very thought of it. This changeableness can make her feel resentful after she has given in to her husband. All this must be taken into account in making decisions. Compromise, not submission, should be the rule. If John forges ahead on one count, Mary must find an acceptable outlet for herself on some other front.

3. Respect for the other member of the marriage association is a must-have. No demand should be laid upon the mate that requires a drastic change of personality.

Nobody can suddenly change his personality at will, and the effort to do so to please the partner is liable to result in a topheavy hypocrisy—a superstructure calculated to impress the observer, but built on a shaky foundation of chaos.

The changes a husband or wife makes in the partner's total personality are in the nature of altered emphasis in the expression of traits already present. These minor changes occur as by-products of active response to the personality of the mate in many small daily contacts, and not as a result of exhortation. Nor are they necessarily permanent. A chameleon

51

changes color easily to match its environment or temper of the moment, but a human being's more lasting change is not so readily made.

Each marriage partner must be proud of the other and let the other continue to be proud of him or her. Therefore you have to respect yourself and act as if you did, even at home. Too many couples exploit the sense of let-down that marriage brings with it. After so long a time, husband and wife cease to feel that they must exert themselves for each other in little matters. Knowing themselves accepted, they lounge—mentally, mannerly, and physically—when at home or elsewhere alone together. Some of this relaxation is a good thing, but it is a mistake to let home and spouse degenerate into nothing more than an invitation to be lazy.

Using the mate for relief, as in nagging, whining, crying, or grumbling, is taboo. If you are tired or irritable, you can rest or exercise for restoration, as in the days before marriage. To pour out troubles or act out annoyance without restraint before the mate is to wear out his or her spontaneity and dry up the source of refreshment you are trying to tap. Fatigue and nervousness, expressed, breed fatigue and nervousness in a sympathetic audience.

4. Too great concentration is to be avoided. Even the greatest love stagnates if it is kept out of the main current of life. To care only for each other is selfishness for two, only one step removed from self-centered engrossment.

This is why the unique value of children is their service as an entering wedge in the close-grown love of husband and wife, a wedge that widens and holds forever wider the unity of love it has penetrated. Other responsibilities, other interests, may serve a similar purpose, though more easily dislodged and seldom striking so deep.

Friends, old and new, have a function in relieving the overclose concern of one marriage partner with the other. If they are to play their full part in preventing overconcentration, the friends must not be limited to those who appeal equally to both the husband and the wife. Common friends are fine, but for this purpose there is special need of friends for either spouse who can call forth those sides of his or her nature that are not aroused by the mate. A brilliant man may be bored by his wife's slower-thinking women friends, but these may be just what she needs as a relief from the high-pressure intellectual life she is leading with him. A stylish woman may be appalled at the slouchy appearance of some of her husband's cronies, who are a necessary balance wheel for him in the strenuous gyrations he goes through to keep the sartorial pace she sets.

The factor that underlies all the perplexities, and most of the contentment, of marriage is its unique degree of concentrated intimacy. Here the supreme testing always comes. Each means so much to the other, each needs so much from the other, that there can be no halfway satisfaction in being together. But there will come a first time when John is too tired to go out with Mary, or vice versa. Do not think of it as a blow; do not believe he or she is implying "I do not want to go out with you because I am getting tired of you." You must realize that it is important to have some privacy of time, if not of space. The wife may be alone part of the day and profit by it. When John comes home at night, he has not had that privilege. His need for privacy must be appreciated, whether he wants to get it by staying at home alone in the evening, or by going out without his wife, or by having his friends in when she is not around.

5. The general level of emotion is what counts, not the spectacular scaling of peaks. Staking all on high moments is melodrama with no comic relief.

Some husbands, some wives, are artists at achieving and momentarily living up to romantic settings, but quickly flop down to the lower levels of decent fairness between the high spots of their sentimental flare-ups. Others cannot utter a poetic phrase, make a romantic gesture, or let their eyes show the quick intensity of their tender emotions if they must die for it. This difference is one of make-up and training, not of marriage capacity.

The couple who are sure of each other's steady affection, regardless of its expression in romantic interludes, are the ones who can afford to smile at the anxiety of those newly married husbands and wives who are terror-stricken at any lessening of the outward expressions of love.

Another terrible moment that is due to come may seem even more frightening because it is you who are slipping. Soon or late you find that some familiar mannerism of your spouse displeases you. It may be a slight uncouthness at table, a peculiar back-country phrase or pronunciation, some gesture of timidity or swaggering. Once you loved it as a part of the individuality of the person you fell in love with. Now it vexes you. And your vexation terrifies you. Does this mean that you no longer love your mate as you did? You cannot help your change of feeling. How, then, can you hope to keep your affection from disappearing altogether if it has already begun to wane? You remember other people you once thought you loved, and wonder, panic-stricken, how you can keep this love from dying as those other loves did.

This is probably an almost universal experience, marking, not the beginning of the end of love, but the passage from an adolescent type of blind devotion to a more mature affection that persists in spite of being able to admit the flaws it sees. For the very young a person must register one hundred percent or be rejected. Maturity brings recognition of human imperfections in the most heroic, but also develops the ability to weigh big and little things and to love with more confidence because unafraid of being disturbed by little imperfections.

Now that you can see your mate more clearly, you should also be able to see more accurately his, or her, good points, which before were hidden from you in the mist of your enthusiasm. Your love is now becoming less self-centered and more helpful to your partner.

6. *There can be no holding on to the present nor seeking to bring back the past. Each moment is new and good in itself.*

The tale is never told. Always it is the unturned page the holds the answer to the question, "How goes it with this marriage?" The present is useful only as a foundation stone for the future, which is being built up out of many fleeting present moments, each quickly lost in the past.

Trying to convince yourself that you still feel a kind of love you have outlived prevents your growing into the more mature kind of love that fits your present stature and prepares for the needs of the future. Attempting to hold the partner to a similar static expression of love hampers the growth in him or her of an expanding reality of love.

7. *There can be no narrowing of marriage to mere sex adjustment. What is essential is life adjustment, of which sex is but a part.*

To interpret the marriage association as little more than sex is to throw away all chance of success, even in the realm of sex. The two lives have to be adjusted to each other, and the two persons have to work out a common life that means something to them over and above the pleasure they may take in each other's company. As a continuing part of this life adjustment, sex adjustment can develop into a permanent factor of married happiness; but without the larger adjustment, the partial adjustment cannot be made in any fundamental and enduring form.

In the sex life in marriage, as in other parts of the association, each partner wins by considering the other before the self. Since marriage grows by enveloping, rather than by being enveloped by, any one element, every part of the married life must receive the same painstaking attention. At no point can the domination of either partner over the other take the place of adjustment.

8. There must be no cultivation of sensitiveness, no looking for hurt, but instead a complete trust in each other.

One who prides himself or herself on having to be handled with gloves has a great deal of growing up to do in order to be able to be an active partner in the marriage. Cry-babying is no more helpful in marriage than in business or social life; it is only more easily indulged in, more tempting because of the sympathetic response it is likely at first to receive.

In the healthy marriage, this sympathetic response will soon give way to anger, which in turn may have the effect of a dash of cold water in the face of the oversensitive one, helping him or her to buck up and behave like an adult. In the unhealthy marriage, sympathy will grow into pity, which drives out the indispensable attitude of respect.

The person who has the backbone to try to play the part of a mature being will realize that getting hurt in any human association is a two-edged affair. Both get hurt, but the weak person does nothing but squeal about it, while the robust ignores it except for trying to take some constructive step to prevent future occasions for hurt. The marriage partner who is mature will maintain trust in the other's good intentions in the face of what might seem to be occasions for hurt feelings.

A chief advantage of the married estate is its opportunity for frankness. "Why doesn't his wife tell him of that unpleasant mannerism, so he can correct it?" bears witness to the universal appreciation of this function of married life. But if John nurses hurt feelings whenever Mary punctures his vanity by suggesting that he presents to the world a less than perfect front, Mary may soon lose courage and relinquish her wifely job of husband improvement. Or the combination may be reversed.

Frankness must go clothed in tact. Stiff-minded people who are frank only when angry lose their case before they present it. If the expression of anger is to have its proper stimulative effect, it has to be administered but rarely, and then in small doses. More has a paralyzing effect on the recipient, producing a response in kind that takes away the ability to think of anything except retaliation.

9. Willingness to grow is the most necessary factor for success. Marriage is a life program of going on together that requires maturity; failure means that there is a holding on to childishness.

We are all immature at some points, but we can welcome opportunities for growth, painful though they may be. The man and woman who find their marriage yielding diminishing returns may be sure they are attempting to hold it to an adolescent level. As this is an impossibility, they are aware of increasing dissatisfaction. That does not mean they are unadapted to each other. They are afraid to leave the known pleasures of their first youth for the unguessed satisfactions of maturity, so they try to stand still, hoping to keep their marriage, unchanged, in its first stage of promise.

If both husband and wife accept maturing responsibilities as they come, their marriage relationship will keep pace with their own development and will therefore become increasingly satisfying to them. A truly mature couple do not look back with longing to the early part of their married life, but appreciate its value as a phase that led up to the deeper content of each succeeding phase.

Having invested years, their youth and hopes, in their marriage, it would be poor business for any couple to fail to follow up their initial investment by putting in such small regular amounts of thought and effort as will make a go of it. The difference between success and failure is the hairline difference between caring and ceasing to care for one's investment.

Married life is serious business, as living always is, but it is easier and at the same time more rewarding than single life. To be human is to be lonely. To be successfully married is to have an inner bulwark against loneliness.

Elizabeth Bussing

CHAPTER SIX

Marriage Makes the Money Go

"And they lived happily ever after!"

The romance in the old storybook always ended blissfully in marriage. The valiant Prince Charming slew dragons, vanquished giants, and worsted sorcerers; but once he had attained the fair lady of his dreams, he left all his worries behind him.

Today, however, Prince Charming, unless he is an incurable romanticist, realizes that the real struggle begins only after marriage.

"Now that you have won the fair lady how are you going to support her?" is the question he must solve satisfactorily before he can qualify as a suitable husband. The answer is determined by two factors: "How much money is earned?" "How can that sum be spent most efficiently?"

The first query is quickly disposed of. The second, however, requires careful thought and planning. Its solution is up to both the husband and the wife, for each couple must work out their individual problem. We wish we could do it for them, but we can't. At best we can only give the rules which we have evolved as the result of our own experience.

The first step in the art of orderly spending is the preparation of an adequate budget. This is not so formidable as it seems, for the budget is nothing more than an inventory of resources and a calculation of needs that will help you develop a schedule of spending which should be fair to both you and your partner. It will differ in detail for each couple, because no matter how similar circumstances may seem to be, senses of values will vary.

At the start, however, it is well to keep an itemized account of expenditures to aid in adjusting your budget to actual needs and to learn just how much you are spending for each item. You may find that you have been paying more for some things than you thought you were. Once you have settled on the approximate amount to be allotted to each purpose, however, you probably will find that keeping a written record of every purchase is more of a nuisance than a help.

It may help you to plan your budget if you study some of the model estimates published from time to time by savings banks, life-insurance companies, and other financial organizations. You who are just planning to be married, however, will find that these statements are compiled usually for families with two or three children. At best they will only roughly approximate your special problems.

Let us consider the situation faced by a young couple just starting out in married life. Generally speaking, if you live in a big city and your income is about $100 a month, you will pay about $35 to the landlord. Rents, unfortunately, are disproportionately high in the largest urban centers, for persons of limited means. In smaller communities, you undoubtedly will find quarters for somewhat less.

Your food, at the present price level, will cost at least $25 a month for an adequate diet—and this assumes extremely intelligent and careful buying.

Transportation to and from work for one person will cost not less than $2.50 a month. Total transportation costs for both of you—if only one works—will be between $3 and $4. Not more than $10 a month should be spent for clothes, and at least $6 must be set aside for insurance and savings. This leaves roughly $20 a month for all other expenses. It is not easy for two to live on $100 a month—but it is being done.

While it is not true that two can live as cheaply as one, two persons who are in love may live more happily if they marry and both continue to work than if they undergo the strain of a long engagement. This problem, however, must be worked out with reference to the particular case, for, as pointed out in an earlier article in this series, it is more difficult for a man to get a foothold in certain professions if he marries before his apprenticeship is complete. It seems obvious that if you are wed before the man finishes his professional preparation, you will not wish to have children for the time being and that the wife will continue to support herself. I have seen many complications caused by the arrival of children before the husband had completed his professional training.

One young couple I knew were getting along very smoothly while the wife was working and her husband was spending his last year in medical school. The arrival of a baby made it necessary for her to quit her job. This, in turn, made it imperative for the man to earn a livelihood. He took a position in a department store where today—ten years later—he is still a junior employee. By now, in the ordinary course of events, he might have been established in the profession for which he was studying.

All young couples, fortunately, do not encounter such tragedies. If your income is around $2000 a year, your financial position is relatively more secure. You may find a suitable apartment in a large city for between $50 and $60 a month—including heat and hot water. The rent in a smaller community will be less, but remember that if you furnish your own heat and hot water, you must add the cost of fuel. If, to save money, you move beyond the public transportation system, you must include the cost and upkeep of a car. But even considering the added expense of an automobile (provided you take care of it partly yourself and thus save some service charges) you may have better living conditions and derive more enjoyment from life than if you lived closer to town.

Your food budget now may be about $40 a month—enough for a liberal diet. Your clothing allowance should be sufficient for average needs—say, $15. Insurance and savings should be greater than those of the couple in the $1200 group. At least 14 percent of your income now should be set aside for these purposes.

If you plan to have children on an income of between $2000 and $3000 a year, you still will be able to live comfortably, but you probably will be happier if you move into a community made up of young people of your own income group. This will enable the mothers to make various sorts of cooperative arrangements for child care, which serve the threefold purpose of giving the children desirable social experience, providing the mother with more freedom, and keeping costs down. It also contributes toward a congenial social life for the adults.

The proportions to be spent for the larger items hold true in general for the family whose income is between $2000 and $3000 a year. Without knowing your individual circumstances, however, no one can make a budget for you in minute detail. The amounts you should allot to various items are governed by many considerations.

For example, there are some types of employment that require more expensive clothes than others, while some professions necessitate the purchase of equipment. Again, the major proportions will change with the needs of your dependents, whether these are children or older persons who look to you for help. Moreover, a wife who confines her activities to the home will do many money-saving chores and require fewer clothes than she would if she, too, went to business. Notwithstanding these individual variations, the foregoing rules of thumb will be helpful in keeping you within safe bounds.

But the proportion of your income to be spent for various purposes is only a small part of your problem. Don't be surprised if your budget fails to balance. Probably 95 percent of those who attempt to budget their family expenses have this experience. The primary reason is that few persons really know what it costs to live. This is due, in part, to the fact that we often confuse *total* expenses with *day-to-day* expenses. Most people think of living costs as the immediate outlay for food, clothing, and shelter, disregarding the important item of depreciation.

The average housewife understands depreciation as it applies to food in a refrigerator, but gives very little thought to the same process as it applies to furniture, appliances, motorcar, clothing, and the house she lives in—if she and her husband own it. When replacement or repair of these more durable goods becomes necessary, there often is no fund available for the purpose. If replacement or repair is made, the budget is thrown out of balance. If neither is undertaken, depreciation sets in all the faster.

In order to catch up at this point, many couples take what seems at the time to be the easiest way out—they borrow money. This may appear to solve the problem, but actually the repayment of the loan throws the budget farther out of balance. Not only that, but a substantial interest charge must be met. To cover such obligations, you will have to curtail your living expenses, and you will find this much harder to do than to save for these emergencies in the first place.

One of the greatest financial difficulties encountered by young people (and many older ones, too, for that matter) is that of making an intelligent decision in the purchase of such important and costly items as a house, mechanical home appliances, furniture, and life insurance. The reason why it is difficult to select these things is that we buy them too seldom to acquire much experience with reference to them.

Life insurance is a subject on which very few of us have specific information. It is as important as it is trite to point out that the amount and the type of insurance should be governed by the kind of hazards against which you should provide. Yet it is necessary to realize that the need of protection changes as life progresses. A father with young, dependent children should carry considerably more insurance than a man with no dependents other than his wife. Consequently, it is desirable to carry two types of insurance: on the one hand, a straight life contract, entered into preferably early in life when annual premiums are lower, and, on the other hand, successive renewable term-insurance policies which may be purchased when temporary responsibilities, such as the rearing of children, are undertaken.

Protection for a childless wife might be limited to an amount equal to two years of the husband's salary. Roughly, the same amount of term insurance may be taken out for each child. The earlier in life such policies are acquired, of course, the smaller the annual premiums. Renewable term-insurance premiums are lower than straight life insurance because in the former there is no cash surrender value. Term insurance, like fire insurance, buys protection—and nothing else.

It is a mistake to look at life insurance as a primary form of saving because, generally speaking, the more the life-insurance policy conforms to a savings account, the less effectively and economically it affords protection against the hazard of death. Buy the life insurance as life insurance and put your savings into a savings account. It is well to remember at this point, too, that if you can accumulate enough to pay your insurance premiums yearly—rather than weekly or monthly—you will pay a lower rate.

The purchase of a home is another difficult undertaking for the newly married couple because the average person cannot tell the difference between a well-built house and one which is poorly constructed. Unless there is some understanding of this matter, it probably will be wiser to defer the purchase of a house and live in rented quarters until one acquires such knowledge. It must be remembered, also, that the upkeep of a dwelling is likely to come to a substantial figure and that the budget may be severely strained if one does not know in advance the actual costs of owning real estate.

Not the least of these items to be investigated is the amount of assessments which are or may be levied against the property. The likelihood of such levies is seldom pointed out by the real-estate salesman. Furthermore, if one's position is insecure or there is a possibility of being transferred to another section of the country in the course of one's employment, it would be wiser to live in rented quarters.

It is a good general rule to pay no more than twice one year's salary for a house; of this amount, not less than 10 percent will be required generally as a "down payment." Then you will have to pay interest and amortization on your mortgage, which, with taxes and upkeep, probably will come to as much as the rent for a similar house. At the end of a period of years, however, you own the house, which is a definite advantage.

Perhaps you have decided, as many young couples do today, that you will both work for wages. The arrival of a baby or possibly some other unplanned event may force the wife to give up her job. If you would avoid real difficulties, therefore, try from the outset to meet the big items—rent, food, essential clothing, and the minimum of insurance and savings—out of the husband's earnings. Let the wife's earnings cover only those items which, though desirable, are less important to your welfare, such as "luxury" clothes, recreation, and items of a similar character.

Any couple who depend on the wife's earnings for such essentials as food, clothing, and shelter should be prepared to adopt a lower scale of expenditure for any of or all these purposes, for as a general rule her contribution to the family income is likely to be less certain than that of her husband. The time to take on additional expenses is after an increase in the husband's wages—not before. Guard against the assumption of obligations which you could not meet if your combined income were reduced.

Simple as this rule would seem to be, I have seen it ignored time and time again, usually with the same unhappy result. I have in mind the case of a couple whom we shall call the Browns. Doris Brown supplemented her husband's salary by giving piano lessons at home. They planned to have a baby and could well have managed to do so with but a short interruption to Doris' teaching activity. But—and this is what so many couples contemplating children overlook—complications set in which made it necessary for her to spend the last six months of pregnancy in a hospital.

Not only did the family income decline by the amount she had earned, but expenses increased greatly. Some of the deficit was made up by borrowing, but there is a limit to the amount that can be obtained in this manner. That limit was reached before the last $150 was paid on the grand piano which Doris required for her work. As a result, the piano was taken back by the dealer.

The Browns, fortunately, are persons who do not give in readily in the face of adversity. They will work out their own problem and regain lost ground. Indeed, they have already moved into cheaper living quarters, not only to adapt themselves to a smaller income but also to work out of debt and re-acquire a piano. Much of the heartache in this situation might have been avoided if the couple had depended less on the wife's income to meet essential expenses.

One of the greatest pitfalls in the path of any young couple is the feeling that they must "keep up with the Joneses." We all think of ourselves as belonging to a certain social group—whether we express it in snobbish terms or not. But we need not on that account maintain a standard comparable to that of a neighbor whom we admire if, in doing so, we overextend ourselves. Intelligent persons are not impressed favorably by pretense.

What impresses is training and ability. Since the best time to acquire these is when we are young, it may be necessary for a while to practice the very opposite of ostentation—self-sacrifice. If your husband is a professional man and you have married early, he may still be working for an advanced degree. This entails fees and—what is even more exacting—time. It means sacrifice—giving up social engagements and many comforts which you would be able to have on your husband's present salary. There is no more basic part of the budget today than provision for more vocational training.

Most of us waste money on nonessentials. We have glass curtains before we can afford them, whereas no curtains often make our houses lighter and more restful. We have fancy trays, knickknacks, and extra little tables that we do not need. The most attractive houses are in many cases those which show no evidence of overcrowding.

How many women, if they look into their bureau drawers, will not find them cluttered with accessories which either are not used or, if worn, spoil the elegance and tidy distinction of their costumes? Buying wisely is an art, but it requires no special talent—only a willingness to learn—and there are any number of books and magazine articles available that will help you to be better buyers. There are a few general recommendations, however, which may be made.

For example, don't buy without asking yourself in each instance: "Do I need this?" and "Will it fit in with other things I now have, or will it require further buying?" Thus a brown coat, no matter how cheap, is no bargain if all your accessories are black.

Another important principle of good buying is: Be sure you know what you want; then buy the best you can afford. The best is usually the cheapest in the long run. It means fewer replacements, longer use, and better appearance from the start. Analogous to wasting money on second-grade goods is the purchase of imitations of articles you can't afford.

Don't buy things that require expensive upkeep. Washing is cheaper than dry-cleaning, and if you have washable clothes and furnishings that can be handled at home, you will not be stranded in a period when you have to cut costs by doing the work yourself.

Buy from well-established merchants. Their reputation is valuable, to you and to them alike. Avoid the fly-by-night shop and its vaunted "bargains."

I have known brides who spent their meager food allowances on useless trimmings. Such ignorance is inexcusable; no woman these days need go without competent advice on food purchases. She has only to consult her favorite magazine.

Most budgets allow something for the theatre, social affairs, weekends, vacation, and travel for pleasure. The proportion of your income to be spent on recreation is a matter about which we must not be dogmatic. You must figure out what you want most. In the first place, recreation requires the allotment of time and money to do things which you most enjoy, and these will differ for every couple. We may easily overemphasize the kind of recreation for which we pay money. It is true that theatre tickets, phonograph records, and the like are expensive and offer a passive form of entertainment, more appropriate for older people. When you are young and trying to be happy on little money, it is foolish to believe that you have to buy your fun. Whether or not you have a good time depends not on how much money you spend but on whether you and your husband are fundamentally good companions.

Have you the spirit of play and the ability to enjoy things together? Then you have one of life's most precious gifts. Preserve it by exercise. Wherever you live, there are inexpensive ways of getting into the woods, picnicking together, walking, swimming, and enjoying all sorts of outdoor sports at very little cost. Such recreation is good for you physically, and great fun besides.

Many young couples spend so much emotional energy on their children that they lose the invaluable habit of running off to play together. Wherever you cut expenses, do not neglect to go off together frequently as you did when you were engaged. No money is better spent than the small fee for hiring a person to look after the children while husband and wife take a picnic lunch together, a long walk, or do whatever it is they most enjoy.

Too common today are people like Mary and Jim, who, in their eagerness to do all that books and lectures recommend for little Peter, got so involved in his welfare that they lost all their sense of fun. They are today thoroughly dull people, no longer interesting socially. Jim has failed to rise in his business, for he mislaid the spark of enthusiasm which made him an asset to his employer. Most unhappy is poor Peter, who has become a genuine problem child.

Entertaining may seem important to you, but young couples are not expected to engage in any sort of formal social activity. Avoid expensive dinner parties and substitute informal gatherings where both the preparation and the cost of food will be slight. If you are original and vivacious hosts, your guests will have a jolly time.

Your budget should provide something for medical service. Remember that the largest dental bill comes after a period of neglect. You should not have to spend much in fees for the family doctor. Select one with care and talk over your circumstances with him in a friendly way. Don't be afraid to ask him what his fee will be. It is a false kind of pride that leads one to hesitate in discussing professional fees frankly and fully. Investigate the three-cents-a-day hospital plan in your community.

No more serious question of expense will confront you than the cost of children. The direct expense for hospital and medical care incidental to the arrival of a baby varies in different parts of the country, but it is safe to say that in cities it will be somewhere between $100 and $200 as a minimum.

However, you need not expect to enjoy the frills of a private room and special nurses and think the doctor will take care of you for a nominal fee; there is no reason why he should. Having a baby is not a disease, and you will not need to have fussy care.

You should, however, put something aside for those extra expenses which are almost certain to occur. During the baby's first year, regular medical care should be provided. Your doctor may suggest a contract under which you would pay him a specified amount to keep baby well and receive his services whenever you need them during that period. Under such a plan you may pay anywhere from $50 to $300 a year. If you prefer to pay by the visit, you take the risk; it may cost more, or it may amount to less in the course of a year than it would under the terms of a definite contract.

It is easy to be extravagant in buying unnecessary clothes and toys for the child. Remember that a baby is happiest in the simplest surroundings and that the only two things you can give your child which are of permanent value are good health and an acceptable social attitude. If you have the sort of home which leads him to develop a friendly, happy disposition and teaches him the necessity of living honestly and sincerely with no attempt to conceal mistakes, you will give him as much as any parent can give any child. It is for yourself and not for your possessions that your children may "arise up, and call you blessed."

It is important to you both to keep up your appearance in order to be as attractive physically and mentally as before you were married. But you may have to be very ingenious in devising short cuts to this end when the permanent wave you planned for or the new suit you hoped to buy is deferred by the need to put some more money into your husband's preparation for his business or profession or by any other emergency which might arise. The pluck with which you meet these disappointments is a measure of your fitness for marriage.

In my own observation, among the young business and professional group I have seen less genuine lack of money than fretful stupidity which was expressed in poor management. A lack of imagination and resourcefulness often paves the way to tragedy. We are living in a fascinating age, but under a complex economy that makes many demands on our spirit of pioneering and adventure.

It was picturesque—daring, perhaps—to leave comfortable homes and settled communities as our great-grandparents did, adventuring into new country. It sounds romantic to live in a sodhouse and wrestle with nature. The truth is that they pretty well had to do these things to carve out a niche for themselves in their economic system.

We young married people may have to live in a walk-up in an unfashionable part of town, but the same spirit of daring adventure and the identical will to make a go of things animates us. If you have that spirit, you can afford to get married, and I can assure you that the rewards of facing your problems and seeing them through together are high. Such a marriage is firmly rooted, and when its buoyant young love matures, its flower is an enduring happiness that nothing else can equal.

Jessie Marshall, M.D.

CHAPTER SEVEN

Children? Of Course!

Nowadays we hear much about planning—town planning, city planning, nation planning. The elder and younger statesmen are going to see to it that we are well-housed, well-fed, suitably employed according to our abilities, and provided for in our old age. Good. This, as I understand it, has always been the American plan. I am sure that no American who is willing to work deserves less than the fullness of the earth. And I shall assume that this country is going to be well enough planned to enable you to raise a family—with suitable planning. For family planning is the most important planning. Indeed, the whole point of national planning is to enable us in turn to plan the nation. The nation rests on the family. Your family rests on you and your mate. What are you planning to do about it? How, when, and why?

In our children we live over our own childhood and project ourselves into the future. Until our own children come along we tend to forget that the world, to which we are now so thoroughly and sometimes wearisomely accustomed, once struck us as a thing of mysterious glamour, promising an endless opening vista of keen excitement.

And yet, if life is to continue worth the living, we must continue to hold onto that early attitude. We must continue to find ecstasy in simple sources. And often it is our children—easily yet deeply pleased, ceaselessly busy with their paints and blocks and animals, ready for every new adventure, never jaded, never dull—who must remind us, their elders, how to get the most out of life. In their love for flowers and animals, paints and song, we may rediscover the submerged or forgotten purpose of our own lives. Or our talent may be for building happy lives from the ground up, in which case the children themselves are the answer to our search for pure-hearted, never flagging excitement.

As for projecting ourselves into the future through our children, reaching ahead through them in order to affect, if possible, generation after generation of people yet unborn—this is a kind of immortality snatched from

69

death and a satisfaction, though composed entirely of hope, that parents prize. Strong-souled people feel that their personalities are worth perpetuating, especially in conjunction with their beloveds'! In proportion to their love of life, to the strength of their joy and the clarity of vision of even better things, people find one lifetime all too short to fulfill the expanding urges within them. In their children they see human beings who may carry on their work, or at any rate transmit their traits to grandchildren and great-grandchildren.

Just at present people who have found life good, the ideal parents, feel the need of entrusting the future to people like themselves, the desperate need to keep power from falling into the hands of morbid madmen who, under the pretext of enlarging life, precipitate horrible wars precisely because they themselves, starved, oppressed, or humiliated from the cradle, have never found life good. Yes, our children can make all the difference between a life full of hope for the future of the race and one of pessimism and despair. It is this sense of children as carrying something of ourselves, our tempers, our hopes, into the future which is at the bottom of what we call the eugenic urge—the desire, that is, to beget good stock and pass on only the best in us.

About the obvious pleasures that children bring, the fascination of seeing their characters unfold, the happiness of festivals like Thanksgiving, Christmas, and Easter, which without children lose half their charm, it is not necessary to speak.

For our purposes, however, the point is that there are literally dozens of reasons why nearly all of us want children. The problem is when to have them and in what numbers. For modern man likes to know what he is about in this world and to direct and control his destiny in the light of other knowledge and experience.

The time for the first baby is a question of readiness on the parents' part. Are they ready physically, psychologically, economically? These are not, of course, three separate ways of being ready; they are interdependent ways, but they offer suitable heads under which to discuss the subject.

Economic readiness is of utmost importance. Insecurity of employment, insufficient means to provide the mother and baby with medical supervision and good food, or looming debts are in themselves sufficient to prevent prospective parents from attaining the other kinds of readiness—physical and psychological. On the other hand, young people with steady incomes should not postpone having children merely because those incomes are not high. Three can live almost as cheaply as two, especially in the child's first years. It is the expense of hospitalization and doctor's care, during pregnancy and throughout the first year or two following the birth, that sometimes threatens to unbalance the family budget. This additional expense must be provided for. It need not be great—a matter of a few hundred dollars, often less in various parts of the country. The doctor's fee for pre-natal care and delivery will correspond roughly, unless he is a senior specialist of great reputation (by no means a necessity for healthy people), to the expense for hospitalization. The latter can frequently be obtained for a hundred dollars or less—though rarely, if ever, in a big city—making the total cost of getting the baby about two hundred dollars. In many parts of the country hospital schemes, into which you make a monthly or yearly payment, make it possible to get two weeks' hospitalization for mother and baby, with semi-private room, use of delivery room, and nursing care, for about ten dollars. This effects an obvious saving, and has done a great deal to bring children within the reach of all. During the first year or so the mother needs to be quite free to call on her doctor for service or advice whenever she wishes. Sometimes the doctor will be glad to arrange a flat charge for a year's attention, say a hundred dollars, or more or less, depending on the family income. Such an arrangement often does the parents a great deal of good, putting their minds at rest, for they feel they can call on the doctor in all reasonable emergencies, ask him all necessary questions, expect periodic visits to their baby, and receive all necessary vaccinations and immunizations for a fee they can afford. The sum may be paid in monthly or quarterly installments.

Money for the child may be saved out of monthly earnings. This well-known phenomenon is called saving for children. Very often the parents of the married couple are glad to help them with the extra expense involved in having their first child. I do not mean by loans—for it is not good for young people to be in debt, even to loving creditors—but by actually undertaking to pay the hospital and the physician. If people are ready for a baby in all other ways and only money keeps them from parenthood, the prospective grandparents often feel it their duty to help in this way. Dr. Josephine Hemenway Kenyon, director of the Health and Happiness Club of *Good Housekeeping,* has often made the wise suggestion that fathers give, in addition to any other wedding present, a $500 or $1000 bond, called "The Baby Bond," to be kept to meet the expenses of bringing the first baby into the world and protecting its first year of life. This idea appealed so strongly to some parents that Dr. Kenyon went even further, suggesting that young parents who can afford it take out a ten-year endowment policy of $1000 for their thirteen-year-old children, to be available when these children are twenty-three, if needed, to help them start their own families.

The question of the right age for parenthood is naturally of importance. But it depends on many factors, chief among which, after the economic problem has been disposed of, are physical and psychological health. Some time between twenty-three and twenty-eight seems to me to be a satisfactory time for a woman to bear her first baby; but any time up to thirty-five presents no difficulty, provided the physical and mental conditions are healthy and propitious. Plenty of women of forty and over have been known to go through first and subsequent pregnancies successfully, but there is no reason for postponing children to this age except failure to find the right mate earlier in life. People who have their first child when over thirty-five are themselves over fifty when the child goes through adolescence—an age which may make it difficult to help the child meet its crucial problems in the tone of one good friend to another. If you cannot have your children before thirty-five, you must make every effort to remain young enough for spiritual companionship with them. The best age for parenthood is to be determined, not in terms of years, but of physical and psychological health and happiness.

In marriage psychological health and happiness are largely dependent on love. It is of the utmost importance that every child should be a love child, in the best sense of the term. Love is a splendor that eludes definition, but it is characterized by an inexhaustible desire for the beloved's company and a steadily burning fire of enthusiasm and admiration. So-called disillusion in love comes from the failure of these emotions. Young lovers, through plenty of courting and companionship, should try to make sure of the lasting quality of their love. This is sometimes impossible, however, and for this reason and others I think it is just as well for married people to wait a year or even two before having their first child. In the happiest marriages there are many adjustments, unforeseen before the wedding, to be made. And it may very well be that only in the continued intimacy of marriage can the strength of love be tested. Only there can love gutter out or prove itself stronger than death—so much stronger indeed, that, as it deepens and widens in fullness and power, it turns of its own accord directly toward the creation of more life.

In other words, the best time to have children is when the lovers, sure of themselves and of each other, feel an imperious need to stamp the gold of life with each other's images. I feel no hesitancy in urging married couples to take a year or so to make sure of their love, if only for the children's sake. Economic conditions being adequate, there is no reason to suppose that real lovers will put off having children until it is too late to obtain the best eugenic results. To paraphrase the poet, we may say that those who restrain their desire for children do so because their desire is weak enough to be restrained. Such people will probably not make good parents. True lovers will beget children after a year or two, nor will they mind making a few so-called sacrifices, as of parties and new automobiles, for the sake of having children. They recognize the distinction between entertainment and joy. Man may be a laughing animal, but he is more essentially a creative animal. His deepest pleasures are simply the by-products of his activity. In building a home around a family of children both men and women often find the deepest of all possible pleasures. And when it is in this spirit of vital affection that the child is begotten, we get, as the eugenists say, a vital fertilization. The chances are that children so begotten will themselves be capable of strong, sound, deep-seated feelings. As Dr. Kugelmass says in *Growing Superior Children*, "The degree of emotional devotion of one parent to another is reflected dominantly in the transmission of the more vital elements in the constitution of the progeny."

To the question of physical readiness for childbirth I come last, but not because it is of least importance. Without physical health the parents cannot expect to beget healthy children, nor indeed can they, in many cases, manage even to bear them. As everyone knows, women afflicted with tuberculosis, heart disease, and kidney changes should probably refrain from bearing children. But this is a matter for the doctor to decide. Such people, if their troubles are not severe, may safely bear at least one child, sometimes two. They should put themselves in the hands of a good physician and rely implicitly on his findings and advice. Sufferers from venereal diseases should not attempt to beget children till they have been given a clean bill of health. Nor should children be begotten when the body is weakened by temporary disease or during the stage of debilitating after-effects. For disease and fatigue affect sex cells unfavorably. So do mental strain, depression and overexcitement. Unhealthy physical and mental states in the parents lead to debilitated or deficient offspring. They open the way to the operation of undesirable hereditary factors which generations of self-controlled parents have been driving into the background and attenuating to the point of disappearance. It is possible for the father, too, to weaken his vitality by excessive sexual activity. In fine, the best time for conception to take place is when the lovers' sense of well-being, physical as well as mental, is at its fullest.

Full-bodied passion, which we may think of as a kind of crisis of love and health, will give us offspring to be proud of. One thing we cannot plan, however, is the sex of the child to come. Nor should we, in general, wish to. It was the limited sphere of feminine activities that once tended to make girls a debit, boys a credit. Nowadays girls have just as many opportunities of becoming interesting human beings as have boys. It is a favorite theory of my husband's that they may, and often do, become more interesting, because they can do not only everything that boys can do but one thing more—they can bear children, a humanizing experience of the greatest possible value.

Should you wish to know what are your chances of having twins, I must remind you that the tendency to give birth to them is an inherited trait, especially through the father. Twins are much more likely to be girls than boys, and to be born later rather than earlier in the mother's married life. Thus it is three times more likely that a woman of thirty-eight will give birth to twins than that a woman of twenty-four will do so. Should you fear that the unpredictable appearance of twins will unbalance your baby budget, you can, for a moderate sum, insure yourself against this chance with many of the larger insurance companies. The insurance must be taken out before the existence of twins in the uterus can be diagnosed—that is, in the first two or three months of gestation. One twin birth occurs to about 90 single births, one triple to about 8000, and one quadruple to about 650,000. In all medical literature only about 30 cases of quintuplets have been recorded. Multiple births are not only rare, but the babies are often so delicate that they are extremely difficult to rear. We can be well pleased if our first pregnancy eventuates in a single healthy baby of either sex.

All the reasons for wanting the first child apply in the case of the second, and to them are added more. What was in the first instance simply a hope and a vague if powerful urge has now grown into a conscious desire, based on the self-knowledge and experience gained from loving and looking after the first child. We have had a real taste of the joys of home and family building, and now nothing short of economic catastrophe is likely to stop us from building higher. I assume, of course, that the mother did not encounter any severe difficulties in giving birth to her first child. If she was in good medical hands, she probably did not, though certain unusual formations of the pelvis may have made her labor longer than usual. I do not say more painful, because medical science has found ways of minimizing the pains of childbirth. Even if it was found necessary to deliver the first child by Caesarean operation, a woman in normal health can without danger bear at least two children by this method. And at the very least a family should include two children.

Quite apart from the parents' natural desire to go on expressing their mutual love by building a full-voiced home on the foundations laid by the first child, it soon becomes apparent that this first child, for the sake of its own social and moral development, needs a little brother or sister. It needs companionship. It needs to share its toys and its parents. Otherwise it will tend to grow self-centered. By being too much with grown-ups it may become moody and negative.

After the question, "Can you afford it?"—and I sincerely hope you can—the next question facing the mother who wants a second child is, "When can I bear it with the maximum amount of benefit to it, to my first child, and to myself?" Clearly, if it is to be a playmate for the first child, you will want to have it as soon as possible. But, in fairness to both the mother and the child-to-be, there should elapse a period of about two years between the birth of the first and the conception of the second offspring. Less time than that will seldom allow the mother, who put so much of her best blood and bone into building and nursing the first baby, to recover fully her maximal physical health and strength. All authorities are agreed on this point. There may be exceptions, of course, and there are always mothers who, by reason of having married late, perhaps, are anxious to have as many babies as quickly as possible. But most women neither can nor will nor should produce children in this fashion. There is too much risk of weakening the mother's body and of begetting poor stock.

Later children may be spaced to suit the desires of the parents, a recovery period of two years or more always being allowed the mother. But will there be any later children? Dr. Ellsworth Huntington in his contribution to this volume has told us that most of us who are not shiftless and incompetent, on one hand, or wealthy and well-established, on the other, belong to a group in which the average number of children, including those who die young, is fewer than three. Dr. Huntington rightly deplores this "rapid fall of the birthrate, especially among intelligent, far sighted, industrious, progressive people whose ideals of family life are high." The trouble with a family of fewer than three is that it cannot be counted on to project very far into the future those sound souls, that good biological inheritance, which the parents flatter themselves are so definitely worth preserving. A family of two or even three children will not, on the average, produce two who, by becoming parents, may be thought of as replacing their father and mother. Thus a family of fewer than four children may be said to be dying out. This is a sorry state of things for those parents who, as I said above, like to think of themselves as affecting the destinies of the race by transmitting their best characteristics from generation to generation.

When intelligent people are forced to limit their families to one or two children by lack of money, it is a great pity. There is a great abundance of good things in America, but we do not seem to be able to get these things distributed in such a way as to do the most good. We are all working for a better world, but are we working hard enough? I sometimes think that we are not working so hard as we might, because our stake in that better scheme of things is not large enough. If we dared to have three or four children, with all the sacrifices implied, I wonder whether this fact would not sharpen our scent on the trail of the better America.

Lord Bacon said that those who have children have given hostages to fortune. But I am inclined to think that those who have made large and important bargains with chance are just those who will move heaven and earth to guard against mischance. One aspect of the better America, proposed by the American Eugenic Society, will perhaps be the adoption of a sliding-wage scale, characterized by a rise in pay upon marriage and with the arrival of each successive child.

That thoughtful people of our time, whether rich or not, will soon return to having families as large as our grandparents' is extremely unlikely. To bear ten or fifteen children would probably kill most modern women or so completely wear them out that the remnant of their lives would not be worth living. And families of this size would similarly exhaust even unusually large pocket-books, leaving most fathers insolvent. Though it is probably true, as economists say, that our land and its resources, if more equitably distributed and scientifically exploited, are capable of supporting many more millions of Americans than at present, there seems to be no good reason for stepping up the modern middle-class family beyond four or five children.

The reader will notice that I have been going on the assumption that people can have children, and fine specimens at that, to order—when and as they please. This is to a large extent true. The key to the mystery is the doctor. Modern medical schools and modern law have entrusted into his hands not only the physical but the mental well-being of his patients. The tight interlocking of the body and spirit has been everywhere recognized, and the impossibility, in many illnesses, of healing one without treating the other. Positive well-being in the body, so important for the begetting of strong children, is practically inconceivable apart from positive happiness in the mind.

Thus it has become a prime tenet of eugenics that babies must not be conceived under conditions of excessive mental worry or strain. Children begotten in deprivation or the fear that they are going to lower the whole family's standard of living to a painful pinch are not going to have much chance, even while in the womb, to turn out fit and strong. Judicious limitation of birth for reasons of health, the *whole* health of the parents, in behalf of the best possible grade of offspring has therefore become a routine part of the physician's service to his patients. Every married couple should put themselves in the hands of a physician whom they respect and admire, making him an indispensable third partner to their family planning. This crucial role of the doctor in eugenics is one of the few really deeply encouraging signs of our times.

The Woman Asks the Doctor, by Dr. Emil Novak of Johns Hopkins, gives some idea of the role the modern physician may play in helping parents plan the vigorous citizenry of the future. When the married lovers are ready to have their children, it is naturally with the woman that the doctor is most concerned, correcting structural or functional deviations or mild organic disease before the pregnancy has advanced too far, seeing to it that the glandular mechanisms do their important work, that nutritional intake is sufficient, that digestion is kept successfully functioning, that metabolic processes are raised to more than ordinary efficiency, and that the body is kept free from all toxins and infections. After the birth of the child the doctor will not only look after the child but also see to it that the mother suffers no adverse after-effects and is restored to her maximal health and efficiency as soon as possible, ready to bear her next healthy baby when the time shall come.

Should a baby be conceived unexpectedly, the doctor is often the best person to help the parents handle the untoward situation. He can give the mother's physical condition that special attention which it will probably need if she has borne another child quite recently. If the objection to the child arises from economic or psychologic unpreparedness, there is no one better fitted, possibly, than the modern physician for changing negative fear to positive desire. By the force of his own enthusiasm for new life, by his vision of the modern family, by a skillful combination of his common sense and psychiatric training, and by his ability to arrange fees within the range of his worried clients, he can usually turn the unplanned conception into a happy accident.

It is often to the physician, too, that the father must look for practical guidance and encouragement in those unforeseeable cases when the mother perishes in connection with childbirth. It is he who is in the best position to prevent the father from unconsciously attaching blame to the unoffending child and harboring an undefined resentment which may adversely affect both lives. The doctor can help the bereaved father to cling to his dream of family life, can assist him in building a happy home for his motherless child or children, or can advise him on problems which may arise out of finding a new mother for them.

Another important function of the physician is to give aid to couples who have difficulty in begetting children. The question of sterility comes up frequently in our time, especially among cultivated and intellectual people. Persistent failure to conceive we term *absolute* sterility; persistent failure to carry pregnancy to a successful end, we call *relative* sterility. The latter is an obstetric problem and can usually be dealt with successfully. So can the former in about forty percent of the cases. We must remember the rule formulated by Matthews Duncan, that the marriage of persons between twenty and thirty cannot be regarded as sterile until at least four years of normal, happy sexual intercourse have elapsed. I have known half a dozen instances in which a child was born after five, six, ten, and, in one case, fifteen years of complete failure to conceive. In these cases no special efforts were made by the couple to bring about conception.

Couples who wish to make special efforts should have complete physical examinations, both husband and wife, for though failure to conceive used to be attributed solely to the wife, we now know that in about thirty percent of cases it is the husband who is the cause. Many remediable physical conditions may be responsible for sterility, and the doctor, by correcting them, has a wonderful chance to contribute to human happiness. Many families feel the tragedy of not having children, and yet do not realize the need of finding out what the trouble is. They just drift along, assuming that nothing can be done, and often they could be made fertile. This subject is ably discussed in *Human Sterility* by Dr. Samuel R. Meaker of the Boston University School of Medicine.

When the doctor decides that there is practically no chance of a couple's having children of their own, their strong family urge may lead them to adopt some. They can find useful information in E. G. Gallagher's *The Adopted Child*. It often happens that people get as much satisfaction out of adopted children as they could have got out of their own, finding cause for pride, inspiration, and comfort in their unfolding toward maturity.

The question of whether we should adopt children when infants or later—at some age under six—is worth considering. It may seem at first glance that only infants raised from the cradle can really take the place of children of our own. While this is partly true, there are drawbacks to be considered. To begin with, the supply of infants for adoption is not by any means large enough to meet the demand. Second, more than half the number of small babies available are illegitimate, and one can often learn little about the parentage. Though various child-placing agencies find it difficult to allocate those children who do not become available for adoption till the age of three or four or later, there are many things to be said in favor of taking an older child. More often they are legitimate and more facts about their parentage can be ascertained; also, it is possible to apply intelligence tests which will disclose whether their intelligence is normal or above. Often those parents who want to adopt children tend to be intellectual, and will find greater happiness in—and give greater happiness to—a child who is of normal or superior intelligence.

You may object to the older child's early environment, thinking that it must have permanently injured even the fairest of capacities. But psychologists tell us that this is not really the case, and that the unhappy effects of poor environment during the first five years of a child's life can be removed, and the child reconditioned without too much trouble. Couples who are no longer young should, perhaps, adopt older children in order that they may stand in the most helpful age relation to them.

Children adopted as infants should always be told that they are not the flesh-and-bone children of the foster parents. This information, which is bound to come to them, will come with less shock from the parents themselves. At the age of five or six, when they first begin to be interested in where children come from, is a good time to tell them. It is agreed that the foster parents should use the word "chosen" rather than "adopted"—they chose their children out of all the thousands available, just as the foster father chose his wife, and the wife her husband.

This attitude toward the question makes for a feeling of family solidarity and loyalty no less profound than that between other parents and children. Everything must be done to prevent feelings of inferiority from growing out of the adoptive relationship: the children must never be reminded of the fact of adoption, the parents must not expect more gratitude from them than they would from offspring of their own, and they must

80

never, never shout thanks to God, in a moment of anger, that the children are not really theirs. To do so is not to play the game. After all, under most state laws, children may be adopted on trial for a year. If the children are kept after that date, the parents bind themselves in law and in morality to bring them up exactly as if they were their own. I keep using the plural throughout this paragraph because I assume, of course, that you will adopt at least two children if it becomes necessary for you to plan in this way your version of a splendid American family—strong, loving, and creative of an ever finer future.

Dr. Hornell Hart

CHAPTER EIGHT

Detour Around Reno

David and Ruth have been married four years. The first few months were glorious: they had to make minor adjustments, of course, but they had thrilling times together, and it was a wonderful thing to have someone you belonged to, someone so comforting and lovable. Yet lately there have been difficulties. David believes in saving money; Ruth thinks that you live only once and that you ought to spend your money—wisely, of course—for the nice things and the great experiences, especially since there is no telling when the bank will fail or when the bottom will drop out of the stock market and you will lose all you've invested. David likes to get away from the house at night—to see friends, and keep up with really good movies. Ruth prefers night clubs and gay parties. David thinks Ruth ought to be more careful about those white lies and those extremely décolleté dresses; Ruth thinks David is rather a prude and mighty inconsiderate in the way he keeps picking on her. And then there is Junior. Ruth believes in loving one's children wholeheartedly and trusting that affection and understanding will bring them through all right in the long run; David thinks that right from the cradle youngsters need to build character and to learn that they have to obey.

Two days ago there was quite a quarrel, when Ruth ordered the new electric stove without consulting David—and on the same day he discovered that she had accidentally overdrawn the bank account! Neither one has spoken it, but the word divorce has been saying itself behind those set lips and those coldly polite faces.

This falling out between David and Ruth represents one general type of marital conflict. A man and a woman differing somewhat in temperament—as any two people differ, more or less—find themselves being hurt by the other's ways of acting. Each allows a sense of antagonism to grow up. This makes them more ready to resent the next difference in opinion or purpose. Once started, the feeling of enmity can grow like a snowball until neither one is willing to believe in the other's honesty, fairness, or decency.

This road leads straight to Reno.

But there are many other ways of falling out in marriage. For example, there is the experience of Henry and Mary. They had a queer sort of engagement. They enjoyed each other's friends and had wonderful times playing tennis and going to shows together. But when it came to love-making, Henry always felt that he had made a clumsy fool of himself, and Mary always felt a turmoil of baffled emotions. Their honeymoon was a ghastly failure. Of course Mary knew that there was such a thing as sex, but her parents had given her a feeling that the less people had to do with such things, the better. Her marriage night left her with a feeling of blind revulsion. She tried honestly to overcome it through the months that followed, but she had to force herself to respond to Henry's caresses, and he knew bitterly that she hated the relation which for him was a deep and urgent need.

In the years that followed they had four children and loved them dearly. They still enjoyed going out together, entertaining their many friends, and taking part together in their church activities; but there was a grim disappointment back of it all, and every now and then it broke out in harsh words which both of them regretted.

Sexual frustration as experienced by Henry and Mary—or arising from various other causes—is a factor in many marital conflicts.

Our next example illustrates another type of disharmony. Helen was really the one who brought about her marriage to William. She was a capable businesswoman, earning a good salary. He was the only son of a divorced woman. His mother loved him dearly; he was her great source of comfort in the loneliness and disappointment of her own wrecked marriage. Helen saw the fine qualities in him and felt that he was being shut away from normal life because his mother wrapped herself around him. When the mother was laid up in the hospital for three months, Helen set about a well-planned campaign. They were married shortly afterward.

His mother valiantly refrained from going with them on the honeymoon—and arranged for them to live across the hall from her in the same apartment building. William felt sincerely that he must not allow his mother to be lonely, and he could not understand why his wife showed irritation when the three of them were together four or five nights every week and throughout the summer vacation. But when he realized that it was not working out, they finally moved to the other side of town and limited the evenings with his mother to two or three a week.

When they first married, William insisted that his wife give up her work, and he also felt that he ought to manage the family finances—with his mother's constant advice. Helen longed for children, and she surrendered her business career in the hope that she might have a family. But no children came, and at last Helen found a new position, not so good as the one from which she had resigned.

She loves William passionately, but she feels that his mother has spoiled their marriage. William loves Helen, but feels that she is unaccountably hard and unfriendly toward his mother, and he is distressed by her insistence upon earning her own income. The mother wants both to be happy and is willing to retire into the background, but she believes that Helen does not really appreciate William; as a mother she does not propose to see her son's life ruined by any woman.

William's mother fixation is a somewhat extreme example of a fairly frequent source of conflict. In some cases the bride suffers from father fixation, and her husband suffers accordingly.

Our fourth case illustrates another widespread type of marriage problem. Sam had had a gay and jolly life before he married. Mabel felt keen pride when she finally captured him from the other girls. He really meant to settle down and be loyal to her when they married. Their passion for each other was absorbing and wonderful for a while. Twins were born promptly, and a year later came another child. The babies kept Mabel tied down rather closely to the home. Sam often found her with wildly straying hair and a mussed dress when he came home, and her temper was apt to be on wire edge after nights of being up with the children. Sam always seemed to be sound asleep when the children needed attention.

Mabel became careless about the cooking: the food was often burned, cold, lumpy, and poorly seasoned. She noticed that Sam always brightened up when a pretty girl was near.

He used to go out often "to play cards with the boys," and Mabel twice found lipstick on his handkerchief.

A nice medical student who rooms next door has now taken to

dropping in to talk to Mabel. She wonders—since Sam is so free and easy—whether she might not also pick up a little thrill on the side. And the neighbors have recently overheard some violent arguments between Sam and Mabel.

Four typical cases of unhappy marriage have been sketched: a man and woman who are allowing differences of opinion to grow into intense antagonism, a couple suffering from miscarriage of their sex life, a vigorous woman married childlessly to a mother-absorbed man, and an overworked and rather careless mother married to a man who is always seeking fresh romance. By way of contrast let us look at a quite different type of marriage.

Charles and Anna have been married twenty years. Loving each other has been the great adventure of their lives—that and having their three children. They always regarded marriage as a partnership—fifty-fifty, they used to say. There have been times of stress, but they have always been able to talk their problems out together. There have even been outbursts now and then when they have got behind on their sleep, and when each of them has been trying so hard to hold down the lid that it has finally blown off. But always these storms have cleared the air, and afterward they have come closer to each other than before. Marriage, for them both, is the great central core of life—focus of love, faith, and joy.

In spite of all that appears in the tabloid newspapers, the Charles-and-Anna type of marriage is far more typical than the experiences of the other four couples whose stories have just been sketched. In almost every marriage there are rich values to be preserved and possibilities of deeper and fuller joy than have ever been achieved. Our purpose in this article is to point out some of the practical steps which can be taken by couples who do have fallings out, to eliminate friction, to keep love alive, and to discover the deeper and wider happiness which might be theirs.

Five Ways To Go

No matter what crisis one confronts in life, there are the following five possible ways of reacting:

1. One may acquiesce ignobly. That means to give in weakly, to "take it lying down," as the boys say. If one is disappointed in one's wife or one's husband, if one's sex life in marriage is a failure, if one's in-laws intrude disastrously, if one's mate follows loves outside of marriage, or if any other catastrophe overtakes one's home, one can give way to hopeless lamentation and self-pity: "There's nothing I can do about it. It's just a rotten world. Nobody ever gives me a decent chance. I suppose I've got to live along and pretend I don't care. Poor me!"

2. One may evade cravenly. That means to run away like a coward. Many divorces are simply a blind and frantic attempt to escape from suffering. Some divorces, of course, are the best possible solution of a bad situation. But quite often the persons seeking the divorce are really trying to run away from themselves. They have never learned how to live in friendly happiness with other people. If they marry again, they will promptly find themselves in new suffering because they have never solved the basic problems of their own personalities. Sometimes the cowardly evasion is mental instead of physical. The husband or wife retires into a private world and puts up an icy barrier against the partner. In any case this type of solution is a blind attempt to run away from the problem instead of facing it bravely, trying to understand it, and seeking the wisest and best solution possible.

3. One may attack vindictively. Most husbands and wives who are skidding toward divorce have convinced themselves that their marriage partners are villains. "This person I married is to blame. He is selfish, heartless, cruel, disloyal, lazy, and nasty. He has hurt me terribly, but I'll get even. I'm going to make him suffer the way he's made me suffer. I'll show him that he can't do that to me!"

4. One may grapple courageously. This means to look the situation squarely in the face, to study it calmly, open-mindedly, and thoroughly. It means to discover the real causes for the disaster, to take an inventory of all the possible resources, and then deliberately and bravely to choose whatever line of action seems most likely to lead up out of the swamp onto higher ground. In any problem which we face, some of the conditions are almost completely beyond our control. One cannot do much, for example, to change the kind of mother whom one's husband has had, to reverse his inherited characteristics, or to cure the economic depression against which he may have to struggle. But certain other conditions one *can* change. Especially, if one will, one can alter one's own ways of acting, of talking, and even of thinking. The courageous grappler accepts without despair the unchangeable

86

factors in his problem and sets about correcting the conditions which *are* within his control—especially his own patterns of living.

5. One may cooperate creatively. This means that one will still grapple courageously, but not as a lone wolf. One will seek to understand the other people who are involved: one's husband or wife, one's children, one's relatives, one's rivals, and all the other people who have any part or interest in the family problem. To understand means to be able to see the situation sympathetically through their eyes, but without losing perspective. Cooperating creatively means teamwork. It means discovering what is the best solution for everybody involved, and then working wholeheartedly toward that solution. The rest of this article is devoted to outlining some practical steps toward cooperating creatively when one has fallen out with one's marriage partner.

If you yourself are confronting difficulties in your marriage, you may find it helpful to note down each of the following steps on a sheet of paper and then write in after each step the applications that fit your own case. See whether you can transpose these suggestions into the terms of *your* problem. If you start thinking about what you face, in the light of these steps, you will probably find new ideas and fresh possibilities coming into your mind as you write. Those solutions which spring up in your own thinking may prove to be just the aids which you need to get a new grip and to start transforming your marriage into a thing of new beauty, joy, and power.

Ten Steps To Marital Adjustment

1. Abandon all feelings of resentment. Emotional antagonism toward one's mate, or toward other personalities in the problem, acts as an effective barrier against finding the creative solution and against putting it into effect. What you hate you cannot understand, because you are ready to believe all evil of it, and unprepared to perceive its good. Therefore surrender all grudges, jealousies, and feelings of contempt. Emotions of enmity distort one's vision and impel one toward actions and words that are not wise. When one person feels resentment against another, the other is likely to feel resentment in return. This intensifies the first resentment, and so the hatred grows. Someone has to break the vicious cycle. Don't wait for your marriage mate to take the first step if this joy-destroying process has started in your home.

Forgive and forget. Let good will take the place of antagonism in your own consciousness, even though your mate continues to carry on the old grudge for a while.

2. Eliminate needless irritants and antagonizers. Make a careful and thorough study of the things that are hurting, distressing, or thwarting your mate. Here is a check list which includes some of the most frequent annoyers in married life.

Stop criticizing your mate—above all in the presence of other people, but also in private.

Carefully avoid every action or situation which makes your mate feel inferior, or which brings him unnecessary failures, even in small things. Don't insist on playing bridge if he a poor player; don't cultivate witty conversations with brilliant people if he feels like a dub in such company; don't throw him into contrast with people who are stronger, more successful, or better educated than he; avoid those situations in which you demonstrate your own superiority over him.

Study to eliminate the topics of conversation which are annoying to him: stop bringing up the subject of his shiftless relatives, the time he went bankrupt, the occasion on which he made a fool of himself, or that political or religious question on which you always quarrel.

Replace those items of household equipment which keep causing unnecessary pain, labor, and irritation: that leaky faucet, that worn-out washing machine, that broken light switch, that asthmatic vacuum sweeper, that torn rug, that decrepit snow shovel, that ready-to-be-junked lawn mower.

Avoid inflicting unnecessarily on your mate people or pastimes which bore him. Don't drag him to teas or to concerts or to prize fights if these events pain and torture him.

Form the habit of keeping all appointments with your mate on the punctual minute. But (unjust as this may seem) do not demand that your mate do likewise.

Never read at the table unless your mate also has something interesting to read and agrees to the arrangement.

Bring your mate into contact with your relatives so infrequently and under such favorable circumstances that their liking for each other will flourish rather than perish.

Do not try that dangerous experiment of flirting with someone else in order to keep your mate interested in you.

Never repulse your mate's sexual advances in a way which will seem unloving, contemptuous, or irritated. If you cannot respond fully at the moment, be sure that you express unmistakably your respect, your affection, and your comradeship, and make it clear that the necessary sexual denial is a mere postponement.

Watch to see whether you are needlessly violating your mate's ideals of courtesy, decency, good sportmanship, generosity, or honor.

See whether you can discover any other way in which you have been unnecessarily irritating or hurting your mate, and make a clean break with that joy-destroying habit.

3. *Find ways to do new joyful things together*, even in seemingly trivial ways. The long check list under item 2 is largely negative. Add the positive side. Buy your mate little presents—from the ten-cent store and occasionally from more expensive places. Make a private list of the small things that please him most (yellow jonquils, Olivia de Havilland, dipped caramels, picnics, chicken pie, Bill Smith, ice-box snacks, Beethoven records, best-seller novels, theatre parties, grape juice with ginger ale, odd china, or whatever they are) and make a habit of springing small but delightful surprises. Cultivate the friendly little family jokes that grow up wherever people enjoy each other intimately.

4. *Have children together* if you possibly can. Have them deliberately, by mutual agreement. Have as many as your mate can wholeheartedly agree to, and throw yourselves into the great adventure of giving them the best possible start in life. Remember that the finest things you can give your children are courage, self-respect, faith, understanding of beauty, comradeship, and the eager desire to serve their fellowmen. These great endowments can be given to one's sons and daughters even though one has a severe struggle to give them good clothes and an education. Often the financially hard-pressed give their young a far richer heritage than do those who are wealthy but neglectful.

5. *Understand your mate.* Set about that job as though your life depended on it. Your married life and its happiness *do* depend on it. Understanding one's wife or husband is far more important than earning a

college degree—and even more thrilling and absorbing, if one goes about it in the right way. Spend time alone, quietly, affectionately, and dispassionately thinking about your mate. What have been his great emotional experiences in life? What are the main drives that determine his ways of acting? What are his deepest aspirations and longings? What are his unrealized possibilities? What are the things that have most thwarted him and kept him from achieving what he has hoped to do?

Sometimes the process of understanding oneself and one's mate calls for expert help. Skilled marriage counselors are available increasingly in our larger cities (but be sure to go only to those who have demonstrated their skill and training by helping other people whom you know and helping them over a considerable period of time).

Sometimes magazine articles will help. Excellent books on marriage and family life are available at public libraries.

6. *Discuss your vital family problems* with your mate frankly, but do not argue endlessly. If there are tensions in your married life, bring them into the open, honestly and courageously. Don't try to convert your mate to your point of view; try to understand his point of view. Try to understand each other. But after you have cleared the air and shared your ideas and your problems do not rehash and repeat and go back over and over again until you are both weary and rebellious. Marriage is a partnership, not a debating society.

7. *Discover areas of agreement*, and develop together joint programs of action on which you can work together enthusiastically. The projects and purposes of a husband and wife often conflict even when their desires and motives are in harmony. Very well, go back of the purposes to the underlying desires, and build new projects and purposes on which you can unite. Suppose that one of you wants to go to the movie down on the corner and the other just hates the idea. Very well; that is a conflict. But if you search open-mindedly, you will probably find some underlying agreement. Perhaps, though you disagree about this particular movie, you both are craving to see *some* good movie; and if you look up the advertisements, you can find one that will delight you both. Or perhaps the essential desires of each will be fulfilled best if you stay home tonight to catch up on your sleep, and then go to a movie tomorrow night. Or perhaps one of you dislikes the idea of any

movie at all, but both of you want to go out for the evening; then doubtless you can find some other entertainment that will satisfy both.

Somewhere, back of the surface disagreement, lies a deeper agreement if you will seek it patiently and lovingly. And this applies not only to a little dispute over movies, but to all the greater controversies that husband and wife confront. Where shall we move? How shall we get along on the family income? What religious training shall we give the children? Shall Mary be permitted to have that Jones boy come to the house? No matter how perplexing the disagreement may be, there is a best possible solution for all concerned if we will seek it understandingly and in the spirit of love.

8. *Surrender nonessentials.* Many a marriage has gone to smash because husband or wife or both clung as a matter of principle to a point which could easily have been given up and forgotten if both had centered on the great underlying essentials. Do not acquiesce ignobly on vital matters. But do not wreck your own happiness and that of your mate over some comparatively minor issue that was never worth the tears and the agony which it caused.

9. *Agree to live and let live.* Cultivate freedom for your mate, your children, and all the people involved in your family problems. To be oneself is one of the most precious rights of a human being. We need it for the fulfillment of our own life. Our loved ones need that same freedom for the fulfillment of their lives. Now, freedom is not defiance of law, but voluntary fulfillment of law. The better we understand each other and the laws of life, the more likely we are to find that freedom which brings the fullness of joy. By one of those strange paradoxes, we never fully win the love of our dear ones until we cease demanding it.

10. *Put the welfare of your family first*, and stop fretting about yourself. Although this rule comes last in our list, it really comes first in the search for fulfillment of personality in family life. What do you really want from your mate and your children? Are you after comfort, security, affection for yourself? Or do you want, above all things, that these loved comrades of yours shall find the road to the abundant life—shall experience richly and grow fully, until they find their true places in the master pattern of our world adventure?

Answer that question honestly. Live up to your real decision. And if with all your heart you seek the joy of these others, your love will be met with the high tide of love, and even out of anguish you will win your way into the meaning and the glory of existence.

Frances Bruce Strain

CHAPTER NINE

Sex Instruction in the Home

A young woman who has won a place for herself as an artist tells the story of her first nude drawing. She was of scarcely more than kindergarten age when, one day before supper, her fancy produced a sketch of her ten-year-old brother in nature's own attire. Pleased with the result, she took it to the supper table and gave it to him—"A picture I made of you."

Brother looked, glanced swiftly at Mother, and started to pocket the sketch. Mother said, mother-fashion, "Let me see it," and then, after seeing, also started to slip the picture out of sight. Father held out his hand. "Let's have a look." Around the table the drawing passed from hand to hand. No one praised, no one spoke, no one smiled. When one of the younger children started to say something, he was abruptly told to eat his supper. Heavy hung the weight of unexplained guilt over the five-year-old artist. After the meal her mother took her quietly aside and said, "When you draw a picture of a boy, you don't have to draw everything!"

"It was years," the artist confessed, "before I could draw, comfortably, a male nude."

Many of the young men and women among our readers, who are concerned with love and marriage, have undoubtedly become aware of inner handicaps of their own—handicaps of thought and feeling which they recognize as their heritage from a generation of other-mindedness in regard to matters of sex. There were silences that caused wonderings, punishments that were not understood, prohibitions which built up timidities, over a long zigzag trail of unrest and fear through childhood up to maturity.

We hear young people say because of their own experience, "I'll see to it that my children don't go through what I went through." And they *do* see to it. Mothers of school-age children, of kindergarten and nursery-age children, mothers of babies, even mothers in their first pregnancies, come with their questions in order that they may *start right*.

At what age do you begin explaining life to children?

How much do you tell?

How much do you explain their own growing-up changes?

How do you keep them from talking to others?

Does telling lead to trying out things with each other?

My little girl doesn't ask questions—how make her healthily curious?

My little boy has a bad habit—how deal with it?

These are representative questions, and they strike deep into the heart of education as we see it today, for sex education is no longer merely a matter of biological instruction. Knowledge of human reproduction is an essential in every instance, of course. It is the basic science back of the whole sexual life. But just as the physical aspects of marriage are for men and women today subordinate to the psychic and intellectual aspects, so in a sex-education program, especially one in the home, biological information is far from being the element of greatest importance. More significant is the guidance and nurture of the emotional life of your children—their emotional natures as a whole, and especially those aspects of their emotional natures which have their roots in the sexual impulse. Frustrations of childhood, failures, hurts, jealousies, misinterpretations of childish love affairs, play episodes for which society has such swift punishment, clandestine sex knowledge—these are the experiences which leave their blight on the later love responses. Life as a whole with its conventions and social codes does not present an open highway to the goal of sexual maturity. But forward-looking parents can, by granting knowledge, understanding, and a sympathetic interpretation of the various phenomena of the sexual life, prevent many of the hazards of the past and provide a better assurance of happiness for their children.

Because the biological aspects of sex teaching are concrete, something one can lay hold of in a tangible way, we shall consider them first.

There is no set age to begin sex education. There is no set place to stop. There is a time to begin, and that time is indicated by any expressed interest on the part of your young son or daughter—a question, a comment, an observation, a wish. The time to stop is when his interest stops. Don't run on ahead of him. Usually interest is stimulated by some incident in the neighborhood or at school—a tank of young guppies, a nest of baby mice in someone's cellar, a new baby home from the hospital, a word in the newspaper. With many very young children, concern about their own origin seems to arise spontaneously. "Where did I come from, Mother?" It is a natural question, yet it has a certain mystical quality, coming as it does from within and reaching back into the unknown.

The greatest number of questions arise between the ages of four and six. After school entrance, questions recede gradually until by the ninth, tenth, or eleventh year children have reached what is called the questionless age. This is not an indifferent age—quite the opposite—but spontaneous questions are less frequent. Possibly they are crowded out by other interests, possibly bits of desultory information satisfy for the moment; and there is always the gradual adoption of reticence which takes place as children grow older.

At adolescence there is a keen revival of interest but more resistance to open family discussion than in the pre-adolescent age. Maturing children are touchy, sensitive, self-conscious, modest, seclusive. They run to cover at too intimate a topic, especially in the hands of adults who are inclined to strike a wrong note; to be preachy and teachy and inquisitive and, in terms of the young adolescents themselves, "too darn sexy!"

No matter what the age, whether pre-school, elementary school, or high school, if questions are asked or interest is shown, explanations are given in accordance with the age, understanding, and general background of the child.

The questions that children ask are as the sands of the sea, yet sifted and analyzed, they reveal a fairly uniform structure on which one may build. It is a foursquare structure of pregnancy, birth, fertilization, and mating, in the order named. They start with a concrete situation—"Where did Mrs. Holmes get her baby?"—and the three others follow in logical sequence. Of course, the pattern varies somewhat.

Well, where did Mrs. Holmes get her baby? You know and I know, yet the thought of getting it all said to this young cherub in a brown snowsuit makes us a bit fluttery. We didn't think that it would. "Oh, the baby. All babies grow inside their mothers." How unbelievably simple! No birds or bees or butterflies, or seeds planted under mothers' hearts. Just "all babies grow inside their mothers." Six words.

Of course you may touch up the story. You will not want to leave it so stark and bare. "They grow in a little place just made for them to grow in.

It's in here, the place is, in mothers," and you give a friendly pat against your side. Many children ask where the place is, and many think it is the stomach. Other children have said so. "The place is called the uterus, u-t-e-r-u-s, and is a little sac that stretches as the baby grows." You don't *have* to say all this. Whether you do or not depends upon your child. Some children, the younger ones, may let you off with a word. Others must have more detail. It's all an individual matter. Anyway, you keep on answering as long as the questions come, and *no longer*. (Sometimes enthusiasm runs away with us.)

We need not be surprised, once the matter of pregnancy is established, to be confronted with a swift second question, "How does the baby get out of the mother?" Sure enough, how does he? About five years ago I put this question to a class of high-school-senior girls and requested written answers. "They are born"; "they leave the mother through an opening"; "they come from the mother in some way"—these were the best answers. Most of the others read, "I'm uncertain about it"; "it's very hazy in my mind"; "I wish you would explain exactly"; "I've always wondered"; and so on.

An explanation of the process of birth is the second foundation square of the whole structure. Pregnancy is the first. One depends upon the other, so we say: "In every mother there is a passage that leads from the place where the baby is growing. When the baby is ready to live by himself as a separate little person, he is brought down the passage and out through an opening into the world. This coming into the world is called being born. Another word for the same thing is 'birth.' Your birthday is your being-born day."

Many mothers like to adopt a bit of drama that can be done with the hands and arms to illustrate their verbal explanations. The pantomime makes the story simpler and helps relieve self-consciousness. "Suppose the baby grows in here," you say, cupping your hands together with the wrists straight and parallel. "Between my wrists is the passageway leading to the outside. When the baby is ready to be born, the passageway widens and lets the baby through. It's a good deal like swallowing, only the other way around. Your food slips down a passage into your stomach, *out* of sight. The baby slips down a passage *into* sight!" There is your story of birth in a nutshell.

Little boys and girls, too, are often troubled at the thought of birth. It seems an impossible feat. So you explain the contraction of the muscles, the size of a newborn baby—"about as big as your Molly Lou doll"—the position of the baby—"all folded up like a little Jack-in-the-box." Most conscientiously you leave an impression of the naturalness of the birth process. Not for worlds would you create any feeling of distress or anxiety. Neither do you, as the mother, seek to appropriate all the laurels. The children do not owe you love and obedience because of "what you went through for them," and "that is the reason I love you so" leaves father a bit out in the cold. No, birth should not be presented as a sacrifice or an ordeal, but as a fulfillment, a joyous fulfillment which mother and father together share.

The two remaining foundation squares, fertilization and mating, take more courage to answer. They strike so closely into the heart of existing relationships. You are fearful, too, that the knowledge will be misused, that it will lead to sex play and experimentation. You don't know how to phrase the answer anyway. There are some things you just can't put into words!

Let's see if one can't, and much more simply than you imagine. Your Philip, or Philippa, who has just learned that babies grow in their mothers, says: "I wonder what makes the babies start. How do they get in their mothers in the first place?"

"Babies are not babies from the very start," you answer. "They have to grow before they are born just as you grow now after you are born. Each baby starts at first from the union of two tiny particles of living matter called cells. One cell is in the father, one is in the mother. These two particles must come together and unite away up in the mother where the baby is to grow. When they do, then the baby begins to take form."

Now for the next step, mating. No, it's not so difficult at all if you have not neglected to build up a foundation for it as you went along. For an understanding of the act of mating, the children must first be familiar with the differences in body structure—that boys have an outer organ, and the girls have a long, slender inner passage. Knowledge of the first they acquired in the come-and-go of daily home association; of the second, when they learned how a baby was born. In a discussion of mating, it takes usually just the merest reference to these structural differences for children to see immediately the mechanics of mating. "Yes, these two parts fit closely together so that the father cells (sperm cells) are able to pass over to the mother and up to the place where the baby is to grow."

To many this will seem a very cold, stark, and inadequate presentation of a deeply psychic experience. In these first explanations of human reproduction, pregnancy, birth, fertilization, and mating, I believe it would be out of place to try to bring about any considerable awareness of either the sensuous or the emotional involvements in the act of procreation. That knowledge comes later. But the feeling which all our first teaching conveys is important. It is especially important in relation to the three major experiences, pregnancy, birth, and mating, about which so much resistance has centered in the past. Our teaching should carry with it a natural acquiescence to Nature's own plan, rather than any outward expression of our own mental philosophy toward it. Most children, given a knowledge of the basic facts of reproduction, usually grant them a ready and happy acceptance.

Those parents who met their children's questions and other expressions of interest as they arose, and also those who were not able to, seek, as junior-high-school days approach, the assurance that their children are ready for that wider experience. "I don't know how much she knows—she doesn't say anything, and she doesn't want me to." Certainly the last thing one does is to probe or question. If you have reason to feel that something must be done, you may go about it in several ways:

1. You may take the initiative by introducing into family conversation some topic of current interest which will promote questions—incubator babies, the Dionne quintuplets, child marriages, the recent thirteen-year-old father.

2. Pets are marvelous biological laboratories—white mice, rabbits, puppies, snakes, turtles. Of course there must be mates and matings.

3. Well-chosen books, not only sex-education books, but simple biologies and Nature books as well, open up thought and discussion.

4. Visits to the zoological gardens, to natural-history museums and art galleries, are valuable teaching experiences.

If the subject is not marred by too much realism or sentiment or moralizing, older children will respond with interest to a discussion of human reproduction. Even when a child is approachable, if your own emotional balance is insecure, it is, perhaps, well to work out these objective and tangible activities with the children, as with a fellow student. The joint interest is a way of achieving in the end greater poise for yourself.

Before we leave the subject of the biological aspects of sex teaching, a word concerning preparation for maturing. In general, experience shows that explanations of the outward phenomena which mark the onset of adolescence—menstruation and seminal emissions—should be made to both boys and girls long before they are likely to occur—at ten, surely, or even earlier if questions arise. Many children become acquainted with them through older children at school and receive not too pleasant impressions. In pre-adolescence the whole matter can be presented so that it is accepted objectively and impersonally. With both boys and girls there is often a feeling of prideful expectancy, and some day you may expect to hear a joyful announcement, "Mother, oh, Mother—it's come!"

At this point I should like nothing better than to leave our teaching to do its own good work for the children. But in the minds of parents there is an ever recurring anxiety—the use to which the children will put this new knowledge. Ideas are not, we know, soporific. They tend to translate themselves into action. Will the children talk? And won't they start experimenting? The matter of "talking outside" is rapidly taking care of itself through the general adoption of sex-education teaching by most young parents. Nobody runs around telling what everyone knows. It has become a commonplace. Occasionally one may caution young school-age children not to say much to the other children, but if they do in their enthusiasm or in a casual moment, no great harm is done. Certainly one does not punish for it.

Children who are overweighted either with too much sex knowledge or with fears and cautions are usually the neighborhood offenders. One father recently told me that he didn't dare give his son the usual terms for his reproductive organs because he would go straight out and shout them from the housetops. As a matter of fact, that was just what the boy was doing with the substitute terms. Realizing that a wooden gun is as good as a real one when it frightens everybody, the child used his substitute terms to shock his father and the world at large. In reality, there *are* no substitute terms. Everyone knows them for what they are, and in addition as confessions of weak courage.

Modern sex teaching is filling the great need of other days in its adoption of correct terms for the functions of the body and its organs as they apply to elimination and reproduction. It is an informal sort of thing which comes along like a little companion of the more important topics. Strange that so much that is visible should go nameless, while hidden things like heart and stomach and lungs should be known! A young five-year-old who adored his pretty nursery-school teacher took constant note of the beauties of her person. Her eyes were so blue and her hair was so wavy and her throat was so smooth, and when she bent over, "you could see her *lungs!*"

In all this provision for your children's understanding, one thing we counsel against. It is the choice of another person—friend, nurse, minister, doctor—to take your place, unless that person has had special sex-education training and possesses those personal qualifications which fit him for the task. A scientific background is not enough. In the near future we shall have college-trained leaders, not only trained but college-sanctioned and selected. Until that time there is no lay person so well qualified to teach children as their own intelligent fathers and mothers. They are able to establish a valued inner and progressive bond of confidence when their teaching has been happily and wisely carried out. After all, in this age of transition when so much is counted good that once was counted bad, and so much counted bad that was once good, it doesn't matter much what our words are so long as they convey reassurance, dependability, and a sense of the rightness of living *with* rather than *against* the best of Nature's plans.

Does sex instruction tend to start misconduct—suggest to children that they undress each other, play "father and mother," and does it impel to too free speech and behavior? No, on the contrary, sex teaching, wisely carried on, has proved itself to be the best of preventives. It has a stabilizing influence and leaves the minds of the children free to turn to other interests. My experience shows a high correlation between sex misconduct and lack of adequate sex instruction.

Usually in childhood, sexual misconduct is not sexual at all in origin. It has any number of causes and any number of guises. Most frequent of the causes are: seeking to know, emotional stress, lack of a good time, sex activity in others, premature sex experience.

Children who do not live in a cloud of mystery, whose mental horizon has been cleared by simple explanations of observable facts—the differences in physical structure of boys and girls, for example—are not likely to be the aggressors or even onlookers in any neighborhood undressing episode. It holds nothing for them.

On the other hand, a child may have a very clear idea of sex differences, may have dressed and undressed freely with sister or brother, and still be active in undressing episodes as an emotional outlet. One such boy was mother-bound. He had been brought up a goody-goody. In order to demonstrate that he was no sissy but a thorough-going he-man of eleven, he headed a gang of girl tormentors.

Sex misconduct as recreation, as something to do, has a long record. In a dull and dispirited world, girls and boys find the thrill of adventure in games, clubs, and play of all kinds, with sex in its most unsavory form as the central theme. A little nine-year-old who had been a frequent offender was asked what in all the world she would like most to do. Promptly she answered, "Go roller-skating." "Which would you rather do, go roller-skating or play 'father and mother?'" With shining eyes she answered, "Oh, go roller-skating!" There was no doubt of this child's sincerity, no doubt of the drab, pinched quality of her meager opportunity for childish fun.

Sex activity often has its origin in a home situation. In these days of apartment dwelling and the crowding together of many families, a child must be very inattentive indeed not to have gathered through conversation and observation much firsthand knowledge of the adult sexual relationship. Children should, of course, be aware of the love of their fathers and mothers for each other as well as for themselves, but love-making in its final forms is baffling and disturbing to their emotional natures, and observation of it often leads to sex misconduct.

The most serious type of sex activity is that caused by a premature sexual experience at the hands of some adult, often an elderly and trusted person. Even if the episode occurred but once, and the offender left, never to be seen again, a psychic injury or trauma frequently (not always) results and manifests itself in obsessive sex behavior.

When premature sexual experience *is* the motivating factor in sex misconduct, most careful guidance is necessary, lest the future love life be endangered. After relieving the child of feelings of guilt, the conduct of the older offender must be explained in terms of his senility or his mental state. "He is not normal." "He should be in a hospital." It is important that this person's abnormal conduct does not represent in the child's mind the natural sex pattern.

Faith in love-making and faith in love partners must be held intact. Yet there should be no discussion of love and no real sex teaching at this critical time. Sex instruction is a post-convalescent therapy. It should not be used as an immediate or first-aid remedy for fear it may become associated with a most distressing memory. Above all, family conversations and speculations should be abandoned, for children are sensitive to talk they do not even hear. A child who has suffered a premature sexual experience at the hands of an older person needs all that his family can give him of thoughtful consideration and reassurance. Yet he should by no means feel himself a hero. Once the story is told and accredited, it should sink into a friendly silence.

Whatever form sex misconduct takes—whether peeping and undressing, playing "father and mother," using vulgar words, making offensive drawings or writing unsavory verses, urinating in public—punishment in any of its many forms tends to decrease the quick chances of recovery. Humiliation, body-guarding (I never can trust you alone), confinement (lock you up), emotional scenes (you've disgraced your family), threats (I'll send you away)—strike deep into the emotional nature of the child and destroy that integrity of spirit and belief in himself which he needs for his restoration. Persistent probings and grillings will also block progress.

Correction of any type of sex misdemeanor requires insight, forbearance, a vast amount of emotional poise, and an understanding of contributing causes. If lack of wholesome sex knowledge is the cause, then wise sex instruction *without* reference to past sins is the remedy. If fixations, jealousies, or a too strict moral code at home are responsible (and they often are responsible not only for the more active forms of misconduct, but for masturbation, thumb-sucking, and other bad habits as well), then the cure rests with the willingness of parents to modify their own attitude and exactions. If the cause is a recreational lack, new activities, new scenes and companions, new interests must be supplied to break up the old associations and supply the needed zest for life. If observation of adult relationships has taken place, a careful explanation and interpretation of the act of mating is necessary to lift the relationship into its legitimate and acceptable place.

The most difficult phase of sex education is the interpretation and guidance of sex activities in childhood. Our traditional codes and sanctions have measured their punishments out of all proportion to the offense. In order to meet this type of conduct constructively, one must avoid severe punishment, the awakening of a deep sense of guilt, and set oneself to work out a quiet regimen of rehabilitation. Best of all, one comforts oneself with the knowledge that, except in cases of psychic trauma, studies reveal that there is little relationship between early sex play and later delinquency.

Wise parents of today build a solid foundation for the sexual happiness of their children. No longer do they withhold knowledge of love, mating, and the renewal of life. They equip themselves with a thorough understanding of the emotional nature of their children and of the technique of presenting sex instruction. We of this generation are seeing changes in thought and patterns of sex teaching and ethics. Codes and sanctions are in transition. It is not that in the years to come we shall have more knowledge or more freedom purely for the sake of knowledge and freedom. It is that we and our children and our children's children, who are tomorrow's men and women, shall live with more serenity, more wisdom, and more joyousness in their love relationships because of the foundations which we have built.

William Lyon Phelps

CHAPTER TEN

Religion in the Home

During my forty years of teaching college under-graduates, if the lesson for the day was pertinent or an occasion afforded the opportunity, I talked to the men in the classroom about their careers—not concerning vocational training; what I emphasized was the right mental attitude toward life itself, the perhaps inarticulate philosophy underlying all choices and all ambitions.

I have always been able to speak more intimately to a group of young people than to an individual. The individual must take the initiative. I believe we have no more right to probe into the secret places of the heart than we have to pick a man's pocket. Whenever a student came to me alone and on his own, then I was willing and glad to discuss anything with him. But I believe every man's personality is sacred: an unauthorized or unasked-for attempt to enter it is the worst sort of trespassing.

In the classroom anything may be discussed without embarrassment. No teacher ever had a more intimate classroom than mine. For my main interest in literature, which I taught professionally, is its relation to men and women. Browning said his poetry dealt exclusively with the human soul; and it so happens that four poems of Tennyson's which, intentionally or not, are placed together, deal with four terrific passions. The poems are "The First Quarrel," "Rizpah," "The Northern Cobbler," and "The Revenge." They deal respectively with sex, mother love, drink, and patriotism. All four have produced happiness, and all four have produced murder. Life is dangerous.

Students naturally wish to be successful in their chosen careers. I told them the greatest and most important career was marriage; that, unlike other careers, marriage was a career open to every one of them. For among the many and striking differences between male and female we may observe this: not every woman can be married, but every man can. There is always some woman who will marry him.

The highest happiness known on earth is in marriage. Every man who is happily married is a successful man even if he has failed in everything else. And every man whose marriage is a failure is not a successful man even if he has succeeded in everything else. The great Russian novelist Turgenev said he would give all his fame and all his genius if there were only one woman who cared whether he came home late to dinner. It would have been well if he had known this when he was young.

I told my students: "Young gentlemen, although very few of you are now engaged to be married and not one of you is married, *your wives are alive*; they are living now. You do not know their names or where they are; but isn't it exciting to think that you are every moment drawing nearer to each other? She is half an hour closer to you now than when you entered this classroom. Some in California are sound asleep, for it is before dawn; some are eating breakfast in New York City; some are eating lunch in Europe. But all your wives are as real as if they were already living with you. What do you intend to do about it?"

Those preparing for the law or medicine take special studies; those preparing for athletic contests take special training. If they did not, they would be idiotic. Those who are preparing for marriage should not leave success to chance. For, while happiness is sometimes dependent on luck, in the majority of instances it is not; happiness usually follows the proper conditions.

Thus boys and girls, young men and women, will do well if they train their bodies and their minds to be successful husbands and wives long before marriage. It is worth it; for they are in training for the highest prize obtainable on earth, and yet one open to and won by millions.

Not being a physician and being ignorant of physiology, I know little about the value of sex instruction. Yet however important sex instruction may be to those about to be married, there is one thing more important—character. Two people unselfish and considerate, tactful and warmhearted, and salted with humor, who are in love, have the most essential of all qualifications for a successful marriage—they have *character*. People about to be married need training in character much more than they need instruction in sex.

From childhood boys and girls find out how children come, but the secret of a good character, temperament, and disposition is not so readily found.

The reason why character is the most important requisite for success in marriage is not merely that it happens to be the chief cause of happiness, but that those who have character can turn an unsuccessful marriage into a successful one, instead of taking the easy way out, and acknowledging failure. No man or no woman is to blame for making a foolish marriage; it might happen to anyone. The test of character is not whether one has or has not made a foolish marriage; the test comes after the foolish marriage has been made. What a triumph then to turn that failure into a success, as the statesman turns a minority into a majority!

This article is addressed to young people, for those who marry late in life either do not need any suggestions or are already incurable. I am in favor of early marriages. I am delighted when either the boy's parents or those of the girl have money enough so that the young pair can be married at twenty-two, before they begin professional study or work. And when there is little money but either or both have a job, then by all means they should be married. When young people marry, they take difficulties of housekeeping and privations as a lark, even as young people do camping out. When I was a boy, camping out was absolute bliss; now it would be absolute horror. Furthermore, in youth neither of them has "set"; they can accommodate themselves to each other.

The late President Harper of the University of Chicago was married at nineteen—not so young in his case, for he had already taken his doctor's degree. He told me that during the first five or six years there were times when neither he nor his wife could mail a letter, because they did not have enough cash to buy one postage stamp. He laughed aloud as he recounted this, and added, "There was never one moment when either of us regretted our marriage."

Marriage can be wonderful from every point of view when it is a combination of the highest physical delight with the highest spiritual development. It is indeed the sublimation of the senses. The great novelist George Meredith, who hated priggishness in all its forms, said in a letter: "I have written always with the perception that there is no life but of the spirit; that the concrete is really the shadowy; yet that the way to spiritual life lies in the complete unfolding of the creature, not in the nipping of his passions. An outrage to Nature helps to extinguish his light. To the flourishing of the spirit, then, through the healthy exercise of the senses."

Could there be a better description of the union of physical and spiritual development in marriage than his phrase "the complete unfolding of the creature"?

To his son Meredith wrote: "Look for the truth in everything, and follow it, and you will then be living justly before God. Let nothing flout your sense of a Supreme Being, and be certain that your understanding wavers whenever you chance to doubt that He leads to good. We grow to good as surely as the plant grows to the light. Do not lose the habit of praying to the unseen Divinity. Prayer for worldly goods is worse than fruitless, but prayer for strength of soul is that passion of the soul which catches the gift it seeks."

What is love? From the age of six or seven on boys and girls fall in love with a good many different persons. But this is not the same thing as married love, which grows by companionship and by sharing sorrows as well as pleasures. Many years ago a college friend of mine, a splendid fellow with everything to make life worth living, was married to a fine girl. He died suddenly, during the first week of the honeymoon. I said to a man of sixty, "Can anything be more tragic than that?"

"Yes," he replied unhesitatingly, "it is more tragic when the husband or wife dies after twenty-five years of marriage."

He was right; the loss after twenty-five years is more terrible; and in the instance I mentioned the shattered and desolated bride was in two years happily married to a second husband.

The overwhelming passion of love is certainly rapture, and marriage is its most satisfying consummation. But true love is not so expressive in desire for possession as it is in consideration for the welfare of the beloved object. "Oh, how I love you!" may not mean as much as "Don't go out without your rubbers on." Do you remember that passage in Guy de Maupassant where the husband said just that to his wife? And they were astounded when the maiden aunt, who had lived with them for years without a word of dissatisfaction, who had gone in and out of the room as unremarked as the family cat, who was thought to be incapable of emotion, suddenly burst into a storm of weeping and cried, "No one has ever cared whether or not I had my rubbers on!"

Yet expressions of love and passion, embraces and caresses, are also essential. I told my students, "After you are married never leave the house, even if only to post a letter at the corner, without kissing your wife." This very simple act is a tremendous preservative of married happiness.

I also advised them during the first twenty years of marriage to occupy the same bedroom. Quarrels and even insults given in the heat of anger are certain to happen in nine marriages out of ten. It is supremely important not to let these flames of resentment become a fatal conflagration. They must not last. Never go to sleep with resentment in your hearts.

"And blessings on the falling out That all the more endears, When we fall out with those we love, And kiss again with tears!"

Although happy marriages are common (unhappy ones are still news), the only ideal, flawless marriages I ever heard of were those of the Brownings and the Hawthornes; in both instances the husbands were men of genius and the wives positively angelic.

Since the greatest of all the arts is the art of living together, and since the highest and most permanent happiness depends on it, and since the way to practice this art successfully lies through character, the all-important question is how to obtain character.

The surest way is through religion—religion in the home. All that we know for certain of every person is that he is imperfect. Human imperfection means a chronic need for improvement. The most tremendous and continuous elevating, purifying, strengthening force is religious faith.

My parents neglected my social training. I am sorry they did. They were careless about my clothes and my personal appearances. I am sorry for it. But I am supremely grateful for their religious and spiritual training. Every day of my life I am grateful. I would rather belong to the church than belong to any other organization or society or club. I would rather be a church member than receive any honor or decoration in the world.

It amuses me when I read novels written by those who never had any religious faith or who have lost it, novels that describe religious training in the home as producing unhappiness and hypocrisy and morbidity, the atmosphere one of thick gloom. As I look back on my childhood, it seems to me that our house was full of laughter. Table conversation was enlivened with mirth. If there ever was a merry household, it was ours. Our daily existence was full of fun, and Christmas, New Years, Fourth of July, and birthdays were delirious.

This is normal and natural and logical. Religious faith is a central heating plant—it warms and energizes one's whole existence. It gives a reason for life itself, for development. It gives a philosophy for conduct, and, far more important, it *emotionalizes* conduct even more strongly than athletics and patriotism.

Of all essential things, the most essential in married life and in the bringing up of children is religion. When two people are engaged and are making plans for living together, they are sure to discuss religion. You remember how suddenly Marguerite turned to Faust and asked him point-blank, "Do you believe in God?"

A chief reason why bringing up children is so difficult is that example is so much more important than precept. I am a qualified literary critic, although I never wrote a novel; I am a qualified drama critic, although I never wrote a play; I am a qualified baseball and lawn tennis critic, although I never was a first-class player. But when parents endeavor to bring up children to reflect honor on the family and be useful members of society, the parents must set a good example. A man once wrote to Carlyle asking him if he ought to teach his little children to say prayers. The severe Scot replied: "Yes, but only if you pray yourself. Don't teach them anything in which you yourself do not believe."

The Scot was right. To teach little children to say their prayers when the parents never say them themselves is like teaching a dog to say his prayers, a trick that seems to amuse many people. To have little children say grace at the table when no adult in the room has any faith is again only a pretty trick. But to send them to church and Sunday School when the parents stay away is far worse; it is culpable. Then the children regard church-going, praying, and religion as one of the innumerable burdens and penalties of childhood, from which they will escape as soon as they reach independence.

When Overton, the great Yale athlete, who was killed in the war, left his Tennessee home to go to college, his father told him that he would not give him any advice as to morals or behavior; "but, Johnny, will you promise me that you will never go to sleep at night until you have said your prayers?" John promised, and afterward told his father he had kept his word.

109

If both young husband and wife share a similar religious belief, it is an enormous asset; and immense help to permanence in married happiness. Now, one cannot believe in God and in Our Lord merely by wishing to do so. Yet I often think that many who do not believe do not really wish to with passionate earnestness; with as strong a wish as they have for money or good looks or popularity.

There are many who say and more who think without saying: "If I only had the faith I had as a child! Then I believed in God and in Jesus Christ and in Heaven." One might almost as well say, "If I only had the knowledge of algebra I had as a child!" Why do small boys and girls know algebra and why in later years do they not know it? Because when they were at school, they gave their attention to it; they studied it; they thought about it. But after leaving school they may never have opened an algebra book or considered the subject again.

What does one expect? If one expresses regret for the lost faith of childhood, it is proper to ask: "How long is it since you read the Gospels? How long is it since you prayed?"

Since religious faith is such an asset to happiness, such a foundation for character and for married life and bringing up children, one might make an effort to recover it, or at least to consider it.

I believe Sunday should be a day of joy and happiness. Sunday afternoon games and recreation are fine, but one enjoys them more if one has been to church in the morning or spent part of the day in either solitary or community worship. Those parents who selfishly seek only their own pleasures every weekend, who do nothing but amuse themselves—are they likely to bring up their children successfully?

To those who have no faith and to those who have lost it let me recommend some wise words by Dean Inge. There are those who are as explosively and suddenly "converted" as was St. Paul; but there are also those who cannot have such an experience; and many, many are the ways to God. Give the matter serious attention; it deserves it. It is the most serious of all things.

Being educated means to prefer the best not only to the worst but to the second best. It means in music to prefer Beethoven not only to jazz but to Brahms. So it is in all forms of art, in athletics, in politics, in everything.

Now, the Person celebrated in the Gospels is the greatest Personality in all history. He knew more about life than Shakespeare. He was the greatest nerve specialist who ever lived. "Come unto me ... and you shall find rest unto your souls." His way is incomparably the best way; it is the way to peace of mind, to courage, independence, fearlessness, to joy. If we find faith lacking, try His way.

Listen to Dean Inge; he is discussing the illumination of the mind that *follows recognition* of the Master:

"This illumination must be earned, or rather prepared for, by a strenuous course of moral discipline. The religious life begins with Faith, which has been defined ... as the resolution to stand or fall by the noblest hypothesis. This venture of the will and conscience progressively verifies itself as we progress on the upward path. *That which began as an experiment ends as an experience.* We become accustomed to breathe the atmosphere of the spiritual world."

Young people about to be married, young people recently married, young fathers and mothers, should give religion the most serious consideration. To neglect it, to be indifferent to it, is worse and more foolish than to be antagonistic. Religion is not a frill or an ornament or a luxury; still less is it a thing to clutch at only in danger or in heartbreak.

Religion is the greatest creative force in the world; it has made thousands of saints and thousands of heroes; it has revolutionized innumerable individual lives. It has changed people from selfishness to unselfishness; from cowardice to courage; from despair to hope; from vulgarity to decency; from barrenness of life to fruitfulness. When religion can change the lives of millions, when it can produce supreme creations in art, it is a force worth serious consideration.

Religious faith has produced the finest architecture, the finest painting, the finest music, the finest literature in the world.

The late John Philip Sousa, the famous composer and bandmaster, said that the reason why there was not so much great music produced in the twentieth as in the nineteenth century was that religious faith had declined. According to him, creation is based on faith. This may be claiming too much, but his testimony as a composer is interesting.

The American philosopher Paul Elmer More, who died in 1937, and who was one of the most profound scholars in the world, after prolonged thought and study and observation, came from agnosticism into a complete and passionate faith in the Christian religion and in the incarnation. He said that while love was the main principle in religion as a way of life, the most important contribution to humanity made by religion was hope. Hope in the destiny of man, in the superlative value of the individual, in the Personality of our Father in Heaven.

I might add that if hope deferred maketh the heart sick, hope destroyed maketh the heart dead.

The most unfair, last word to describe religious faith is the word anesthetic. Religious faith is a comfort to the old, the sick, and the suffering; but in general it is not a sedative, it is a tonic. It is a dynamo; it is a driving force. Henry Drummond, the most effective speaker on religion I can remember, said to a group of students: "I ask you to become Christians not because you may die tonight but because you are going to live tomorrow. I come not to save your souls, but to save your lives."

Religion adds an enormous zest to daily life; it makes everything interesting. It keeps alive the capacity of wonder. I myself am interested in everything in the world, from a sandlot ball game to the nebula in Orion. The mainspring of my existence, the foundation of my happy and exciting life, is Christian faith.

I suggest to those recently married and those about to be married that they are entering into a relationship that can bring them the highest and most lasting happiness or the most crushing disillusion and despair. Such a relationship is particularly remarkable because of its intimacy, an intimacy far transcending that of friendship, love of parents, or any earthly emotion. As Thomas Hardy said, marriage annihilates reserve. In this amazing intimacy every care should be taken to insure success. A common interest in religion, saying prayers together, will help enormously toward increasing and preserving happiness.

For a true belief in the Christian religion will improve daily manners. Husband and wife will not take each other for granted; they will not become stodgy or commonplace or stereotyped.

Tennyson gave in "The Princess" the real kind of marriage which one of my students described in the vernacular: "I am going to be married. It

112

won't be much of a wedding, but it will be a wonderful marriage." Listen to Tennyson:

"For woman is not undevelopt man, But diverse. Could we make her as the man, Sweet Love were slain; his dearest bond is this, Not like to like, but like in difference. Yet in the long years liker must they grow; The man be more of woman, she of man; He gain in sweetness and in moral height, Nor lose the wrestling thews that throw the world; She mental breadth, nor fail in childward care, Nor lose the childlike in the larger mind; Till at the last she set herself to man, Like perfect music unto noble words."

A wife may be a civilizing force; this is well. But she may be far more than that. She may be a revelation in daily intimacy more unconsciously impressive than a professional saint.

This is what *Caponsacchi* said of an imagined union with *Pompilia*, in Browning's "The Ring and the Book":

"To live, and see her learn, and learn by her, Out of the low obscure and petty world— Or only see one purpose and one will Evolve themselves i' the world, change wrong to right; To have to do with nothing but the true, The good, the eternal—and these, not alone In the main current of the general life, But small experiences of every day, Concerns of the particular hearth and home: To learn not only by a comet's rush But a rose's birth, not by the grandeur, God, But the comfort, Christ."

Stanley G. Dickinson

CHAPTER ELEVEN

It Pays to be Happily Married

Business believe that the happily married man will occupy a bigger position in the business world than will the man who is unhappy at home. The young men and young women in *Good Housekeeping's* marriage-relations course have a right to know this, to know precisely the interest which business has in harmonious marriage and the extent to which home life is a factor when men are considered for promotion, employment, or transfer—any one of which means more income, more responsibility, and an opportunity to live more fully.

Business might very logically take another view. It *might* believe that the single man is the better employee, because single men are free to travel, are not burdened with the expenses of a family, do not run the risk of going home to trouble. It *might* believe that the home experiences and environment of the people it hires are not its concern. But business is concerned with these aspects and young people should know in what way and why.

While business negotiates with the husband, it has long since learned that *both* husband and wife are entitled to consideration whenever one is being employed or promoted. The more important the job, the more important it becomes to determine whether husband and wife have tried to keep pace with each other, or whether there is discord at home. Business can afford to place responsibility upon the mentally capable, energetic, and tactful man *if* his marriage relations are harmonious. It cannot afford to gamble with the man who is in trouble at home—not necessarily vicious trouble, but trouble arising from carelessness, maladjustment, and misunderstanding.

As a business consultant advising corporations upon their major objectives and policies, I attend several times each week conferences during which men are discussed for promotion, transfer to new work or new territory, salary adjustments, and sometimes demotion. The business consultant prefers to limit his counsel to such objective matters as plans and operating policies, but this cannot be done actually, because all business

114

situations must be resolved into the persons in them. Hence our discussion is necessarily devoted to men—to what we can do to make them more effective, to how soon we can promote them safely, to how much responsibility they can assume, to what they are best fitted for doing, and the like. During the past fifteen years, I have discussed such lowly functions as clerkships at $85 a month and such exalted positions as vice-presidencies at $20,000, with the average running between $4000 and $10,000 a year.

The judgment of executives is not infallible, and some of the men we pick are unable to measure up to the increased load we place upon them. We try to analyze these failures even more carefully than we analyze the successes. Here is what we find: in the majority of instances, men do not fail because they do not know enough, or because they are lazy; they fail because business cannot always depend upon them—they break at the wrong times. We can find men who know their work and who are capable of learning the requirements of a better job. We can find plenty of men who are willing to work, and who will work even harder for the promise of a better job in the future. But we cannot find enough men whose emotional mechanism is dependable—at least not in sufficient numbers to carry on the responsibilities which business would like to place upon them.

Peculiarly enough, the results of emotional instability are complex, but the chief cause may be defined simply: trouble at home causes more emotional upsets, more instability in business, than any other single factor. By the same token, lack of progress in business causes trouble at home. No home can be run successfully without a degree of financial progress, and such progress cannot be made—except by a negligible few—without harmony at home.

All wives have, by and large, an equal stake with their husbands in their husbands' material progress. The increased income is a major consideration, but it is only the beginning in a chain of useful consequences. Business progress means mental growth, added intelligence to be applied to both working and living. Personal growth means a fuller home life, a finer environment in which to bring up children, an opportunity to become a respected member of the community. Business progress means greater responsibility, and this breeds the ability to take on still more responsibility, both at home and in business. Progress eventually brings more leisure, more

115

culture, and more of the other refinements of living. Progress is accelerating, feeding upon and multiplying itself.

No one would deny the truth of all this, yet only a searching few have actually created at home the degree of harmony which has been the aim of this series in *Good Housekeeping's* course on marriage relations. If effective contributions from home to the consistent progress of breadwinners were universal rather than rare, half of our troubles in finding men for added responsibility would be over. The majority of men dissipate their energy in *wishing* and *wanting*, but restrict themselves to wishing and wanting the *result*, rather than the *cause*. These insist that they want to better their situations, but insist also that business is a thing apart, something to be shut in the office, something which need not be understood or supported at home, and certainly something over which a wife at home has little influence. These two points of view are not reconcilable; hence everyone loses who tries to hold to both at once.

If you say to a business executive, "Business is a thing apart," he will point out at once that your theory is true only in the least important jobs. The management does not worry much about the home environment of the beginner upon whom no real responsibility rests, but it frequently goes to unbelievable ends to get its more important employees back onto the track if they have lost their heads over a home problem. Again, business does this for no humanitarian reasons; it takes this attitude because its employees produce better where there is harmony at home.

The capable, intelligent, and progressive worker is almost invariably married to a capable, intelligent, and progressive woman. Each acts and reacts upon the other. Men are not so versatile that they can fill $5000 jobs during the day and then go home to become husbands of $1500 women in the evening. Neither are women so versatile that they will remain in contented harmony with husbands who are not their mental equals. Some look negatively at the problem, feeling that "I could have done better if I had had the advantages of so-and-so." The facts are that these envied couples were growing up together, keeping pace mentally, long before the promotion came which is given the credit for their present condition.

When a wife falls down on her part of the job, neglecting either harmony or her personal development, her husband's first natural reaction is to separate his business from his home life—to grit his teeth and go on, hoping to achieve the impossible. This usually sets up a vicious circle of events. Being handicapped in personal effectiveness, he spends more and more time at business. His home goes to ruin; he suffers the most dangerous emotional upsets; his work fails, and conditions get worse and worse. He breaks, in short, at the wrong time—a time inconvenient to business, to put it brutally.

It is dangerous to generalize here, because there is a fine distinction between harmony at home and bringing business into the home. Hasty thinking is likely to confuse the two. The man who takes petty troubles of the routine day home to his wife is a weakling, and business cannot consider him for increased responsibility. The husband who takes none of his problems home is frequently a mystery to his wife, but he probably feels that she is not sufficiently informed to be useful in helping him make decisions on purely business issues. Wives sometimes rebel against this, because they do not make the essential distinction between respect for them as individuals and respect for their information about a specific business question.

The soundness of the belief that wives have a specific and clearly defined responsibility here is verified by the fact that *husbands want, and business demands, one and the same thing.* The approach is different, because the husbands of America are asking primarily for harmony at home, while business is looking for an efficient producer; yet they both are seeking the same thing. The husband asks his wife for harmony at home and a progressive instinct so that she will grow concurrently with him. Business, when evaluating men for promotion, asks whether there is harmony at home so that this man will be free from the greatest single source of emotional unbalance, and whether this man and his wife have demonstrated the ability to grow in the past—the best available indication of their ability to grow in the future. These two questions take in a lot of territory, but the ground must be covered so long as business, in effect, employs or promotes both husband and wife.

Do not be misled for a moment respecting the importance of these two points merely because businessmen do not talk a lot about them. Their sense of good taste makes them hesitate to inquire bluntly into so personal a problem, and so their investigations are conducted quietly. Numerous confidential sources of information are used, and superiors take their own means to meet husband and wife together, generally under some casual pretext. If we could look behind the scenes, we would find that emotional stability—that elusive product of a satisfactory home environment—is regarded just as highly as knowledge, experience, or any of the other orthodox considerations. We would find executives saying, "We can count on Jones for Chicago now that we have seen his wife and determined to our satisfaction that she will measure up to the promotion" or "It's too bad we can't give this job to Smith, but you know how hard it is to succeed without support from home." Another would be saying, "Brown flew off the handle again yesterday; it must have started at the breakfast table."

Wives, if you can be the Mrs. Jones of these examples, and avoid being the Mrs. Smith or the Mrs. Brown, you will be removing for businessmen the greatest hurdle to promotion which we encounter. You will be doing your part as the wife of a man in business.

You may determine the extent to which you are doing these things now by testing yourself in the light of these ten questions:

1. Did my husband start for work this morning in a better frame of mind for having married me, or would he have been happier as a single man or married to someone else?

Remember, as you ask this question and apply your own answer, that we are talking about business; hard, practical business where intentions do not count. You may love your husband dearly, but if the results of your love are not constructive, you must write the word FAILURE across the record.

2. Do I always treat my job just as seriously as if I were working in an office for a monthly salary?

Some wives feel that it makes no difference if they linger so long over bridge or cocktails or shopping or whatever in the afternoon that they are unable to prepare a suitable meal for their husbands in the evening.

3. Have I grown in poise and interests like the wives of my husband's associates and superiors?

Wives who keep up with the procession are an asset; those who fail to grow are a liability.

118

4. Can I talk in the same terms as his associates and their wives?

This indicates how carefully you have maintained your interest in the source of your income, and how accustomed you are to expressing yourself.

5. Do I dress and act like the wives of the business associates and superiors of my husband?

You place a heavy handicap upon your effectiveness if your husband cannot be proud of you in the inevitable comparisons with other wives in his organization.

6. Do I entertain with reasonable frequency the people who are in a position to help my husband in business, or is our social life planned wholly for my own amusement?

Perhaps this question should read, "How long since I have entertained So-and-So?" You may be surprised to find that months have slipped away without your having done a single stroke of good for your husband socially.

7. Do I limit our social engagements during the week to those which will not take essential energy from the job, or do I feel that my husband "owes" me constant amusement when he is not actually at the office?

As employers pile responsibility upon your husband, more and more care must be used in the allocation of time to social affairs. You may be able to rest the next day, but business does not permit husbands to rest on the job.

8. Do I act as a balance wheel, cheering him intelligently when he is tired or discouraged, or do I rub him the wrong way on such occasions?

If your husband does not share with you his disappointments, it is almost invariably because you have not qualified yourself to share them.

9. Do I try to smooth things out after unpleasant discussions—as I would if a new dress or theatre party were at stake?

Many married persons have an uncanny capacity for making miserable the objects of their affection. It is said that the course of true love

119

never did run smooth, but the wise husband or wife will not unnecessarily roughen it.

10. Do I carry my share of responsibility, or do I save up all the petty annoyances for our dinner-table conversation?

Wives who complain that their husbands are silent during dinner have usually good reason to overhaul the quality of their own conversation. Don't bore him with your fight with the grocer or the catty things Mrs. X said at bridge or afternoon tea.

Here are some actual examples of the way wives affect their husband's business:

We selected Blake for a branch managership at Chicago, and we thought that his wife could measure up. We took him out of a job where he had reached his limit and placed him in one where his developed ability might enable him to earn twice his salary. He failed. We who appointed this man took the blame for his failure, because *business recognizes no alibis.* As usual, it wasn't that he didn't want to be a branch manager, or that he didn't know enough, or that he wasn't willing to work hard enough. We found that the trouble was within his emotional mechanism. He was losing his head and his temper at the wrong times.

At last he wrote to his firm: "This town takes the heart out of my wife. She is terribly lonesome, refuses to make new friends, and reminds me continually of the good times we used to have back home. Her mother misses her and threatens to come to live with us here. I appreciate this opportunity, and I know that we have more of everything here than we had back home, but I want my old job back. I can't stand it here."

Business doesn't work that way, and so we persuaded another employer to "hire him away" without his knowledge, thus saving his face and helping to maintain his courage. He would have been branded for life if we had permitted him to crawl back to his old job. Blake will never go as far as he is entitled to go, because Mrs. Blake places her own feelings above any other consideration, and her husband is not strong enough to control his emotions where his wife is concerned. Few men are.

We do not in any way blame Mrs. Blake for the part she played in her husband's failure. She merely attaches more value to staying in her old groove, in the constant companionship of her mother, and in the regular contact with old friends than she attaches to promotion for her husband. We have no quarrel with her choice, if only she realizes that she has chosen something for herself, and is now living under conditions dictated by her own choice.

Take Smith. In the language of business he is a "whipped puppy." Again, there is no question of his ability, his desires, or his willingness to work. We have, in a certain corporation, a job for Smith which would mean a 50 percent increase in salary, a place of notice in the community, and a wider acquaintance among substantial people. We have considered him for this job a dozen times, but each time we have decided to postpone action, because we are afraid of the influence of his wife. On his present job, it does no great damage for her to be so possessive, demanding all his time outside of office hours, ordering him around like a child. On the new job, such a performance would ruin him before he was fairly started. Dare we depend on her ability and willingness to grow quickly into the person she would have been training to become? We dare not, for we are held responsible for results!

"Just as I thought," some will say, "business is inhuman." One who takes this attitude has an incomplete view of the facts. If business were to tolerate a repetition of mistakes, its general level of productivity—which, in turn, means income to its employees—would be lowered immediately. This would operate against the very thing we are trying to sponsor—increased responsibility and more full living for all as soon as they earn it.

This point of view frequently gives women no end of mental trouble, because they are more inclined than men to think subjectively rather than objectively. Business employs a man for what he can produce, other things being equal. So long as he is morally sound and honest, business cares little about his attitudes on other subjects. Wives measure their husbands by their helping with the housework or their thoughtfulness in little things around the home; all of these have their value, but not in the scale of production on the job. Sentiment counts heavily with the feminine mind, as it should, whereas business is more realistic. Business buys results rather than intentions.

Business did not have an inherent desire to consider marriage relations. Its interest in them began with the many examples of maladjustment to which it was compelled to give attention, in line with its age-old policy of believing that "everything is all right until it is proved otherwise." When the negative consequences were brought to light, and business really became interested, a constructive attitude was developed which gained its momentum from the countless examples where wives have been major reasons for the success of their husbands. Fortunately for every failure there are a dozen successes.

The Mortons, for example, are a couple who have found that it pays to live both harmoniously and progressively at home. Mary Morton is a convert to the constructive attitudes brought out by the ten questions outlined earlier. They have made it a custom to entertain at least one evening a week, always having in mind that certain people can be *both* good company and helpful in business. They try to reach up rather than down in the people with whom they mingle. When they were to be transferred to another city, the news was broken to them together in their home by a superior. Mary's first and genuine reaction was, "It will be fine to make new friends and to have the children see a new part of the country."

When they arrived at the new city, the old process, so successful in their home town, was begun again—new friends, new interests, new growth. If they were ever homesick, the firm never found it out; but I am inclined to believe that they were too busy on constructive matters to get homesick. Morton's salary is three times what it was ten years ago, and most of the credit goes to his wife. Likewise she is the chief beneficiary.

Another illustration of the extent to which business recognizes the principle of harmonious development of both husband and wife is shown by the experience of Parsons. He was a junior executive, capable in every direction but one. When a vacancy occurred higher up, he was the logical candidate; but the president of the company refused to promote him until he had had a chance to demonstrate his ability to meet the social requirements of his position. He conceded Parsons' brilliance, his energy, and everything but his capacity to become genuinely interested in the people who were both above and beneath him in the organization. Inquiry revealed that he was making the best of a situation in which neither he nor his wife had realized the importance of social activity. Bear in mind that we do not mean a playboy temperament or a mercenary attitude, but rather a genuineness in human contacts.

When the problem was laid before them, a program was laid out for them to follow. Parsons and his wife called on everyone they felt should not be neglected, later inviting to their own home those who seemed in a position to help them. During these second visits, the conversation was turned to what might be done by "people like ourselves" to prevent getting into a rut. Dozens of helpful activities were recommended, and they made it a business to explore the most valuable, so that they could tell others about forthcoming meetings of discussion groups, plays, lectures, and the like. Within six months, they had entirely overcome the president's objection, and a year later Parsons was promoted to the other position at a $2000 increase in salary.

Two facts will occur immediately to anyone who is an intelligent observer of such things: first, Parsons and his wife had a better time after the change than before; and second, business expects people to discover these things for themselves. This couple were more than usually fortunate to be led by the hand up to this new experience.

Business gave Parsons his chance when it permitted him to demonstrate his ability. Quick jumps in business are not made available to people upon the basis of their belief that they can qualify. Business would be guilty of rash speculation with its funds if positions were given to any except those who had demonstrated their qualifications in advance. Business has no time for or patience with those who do not recognize the importance of these things. We have no license to give responsibility to those who say: "I didn't know that this was important. Give me a trial, and I will do my best to learn quickly." The answer to that is: "We have another man who has been qualifying for many years. He saw the place of these things in business progress. We'll risk our money on him."

When a young man brings to business a reasonable amount of ability and energy, reinforced by the emotional balance which comes from the right kind of home life, he is likely to surpass both his own expectations and those of his employers. Business *wants* him to succeed. Business wonders, as a matter of fact, why more people do not succeed, with the incentives for success so generally open to public view. It realizes, just as you will realize when you analyze the situation, that the incentives have been understood, but the ways and means have been missing. This is a common mistake in human progress. We have all erred in making someone else want something, thinking that the process of arousing desire would insure intelligent action. Most humans realize that they lack the ways and means, a realization which accounts for the interest shown everywhere in better marriage relations and in the methods for achieving them. The desire to succeed is not enough. Desire has its place, however, once the ways and means are understood, because strong desire sustains interest in the ways and means.

Does this seem an idle theory? Not to business, the instrument through which most men and women work out their economic security. Business says: you must show us harmony at home and mental growth before we will believe that you are a safe candidate for promotion. Give us these along with the ability you have always brought us, and we will make it worth your while. We will increase your salaries. We will put you into jobs where you may live in better neighborhoods, mingle with more capable people in business and at home, give your children advantages you may never have had, and provide you with all the creature comforts for successful living, a base upon which you must build your own philosophy of happiness, but without which no genuine happiness is probable.

Being composed of realists, business does not paint these rewards in glowing colors. It merely says, without question or qualification, *the happily married man will occupy a bigger position with us than the man who is unhappy at home.*
Ernest R. and Gladys H. Groves

CHAPTER TWELVE

The Case for Monogamy

If we put off examining the case for monogamy until we had personal questions about it, most of us would never get around to studying it. For most people no more doubt that monogamy is the best possible program than that good health is better than bad. To argue such a matter seems strange.

But there is much loose talk about on the other side of the case, crying up the non-monogamous program practiced by a few and publicized by more. The adherents of this group are so vocal that their ideas are constantly being aired. Knowing themselves a small minority, with the burden of proof against them, they excitedly attack the existing order.

Their arguments are likely to interest the average person, however, only when he or she is momentarily thrown off balance by an emotional upheaval of one sort or another. And right there is the danger. It is hard for anyone—particularly a young person—to make a rational decision when his thinking is colored by his emotions; his tendency is to use his intellectual processes merely to justify what he wants to do at the moment, and not to search out the truth. If he is unprepared for the anti-monogamy arguments ready and waiting for him, he is likely to accept them without question. Before we have occasion to doubt it, therefore, those of us who take monogamy as a matter of course should understand why we do, and what its significance is to us. Then, if ever the occasion does arise, we shall be better able to let our minds, not our passions, decide the issue for our greater happiness.

The question is shall I, having given myself to one man or one woman, abide by the till-death-do-us-part vow, or shall I be free to change partners at will?

The natural mood of most men and women entering marriage is deeply monogamous. The one thing husband and wife crave is to depend only on each other forever. Yet later on some of them will suddenly desert the standards of monogamy without giving themselves time to think, and others will pass through a period of turmoil before making up their minds to go or to stay. What has happened in the marriage experience to change these individuals who were strong for monogamy into men and women either dead set against it or very doubtful about it?

The answer lies both in the particular temperament of the persons concerned and in certain characteristic features of the early, middle, and later stages in married life. Sometimes a young man or woman bolts from the tenets of monogamy in a late-adolescent panic when marriage responsibilities begin to be irksome. Sometimes it is the older man or woman who married in good faith only to lose sight of the values of monogamy. Not having the backbone to accept what comes and do something about it, this type of person wants to give up as soon as the going gets rough, and daydreams about making a better start elsewhere.

What are the parts of the marriage experience that bring out this disposition of wanting to run away in order to try again? The romantic love that marks the early part of marriage is a characteristically youthful attitude. Each spouse idealizes the other and pictures their life together as something almost unique in its perfection. Stimulated by the mate's expectations, each one rises about his or her previous habits of behavior, and for a while the two seem indeed to be finer and better than the general run of humankind.

In time the first flush of enthusiasm wears off, and the husband and wife gradually get to see each other more nearly as other people see them. For those who flinch from reality, this is as bitter an experience as any of the other hard parts of growing up. For nobody is it easy. But for all who face it squarely, it is a big step toward emotional maturity.

Without hastening the process, and thereby losing most of its benefits, one can learn to accept it little by little, as it comes. The wife who seemed the most beautiful or most gracious woman imaginable, the husband who was looked upon as the strongest or cleverest man in the world, slowly loses this impossible glamour and shrinks to the life size proportions of a real man or woman.

When one catches a glimpse of oneself in the estimation of the newly married spouse, and realizes how far the idealized picture is from the somber reality one has grown up with, it is easy to think, "I am made different by this

126

love that expects so much of me, and if I am not yet quite so wonderful as my beloved thinks me, I shall soon become so, for this expectation spurs me to hitherto unimaginable efforts."

Something of this improvement does take place—but then, to the chagrin of the one trying to improve, it becomes increasingly clear that the original expectations of the mate are being lowered in the direction of one's actual present level of attainment. Surprisingly enough, by the time one is sure of this, it is not disturbing in the way one would have expected, for one's own impression of the mate is also coming down to earth.

At first this descent from the clouds of fanciful exaggeration of the loved one to the lesser status of everyday life seems more or less tragic, as both fear that the supreme quality of their marriage is vanishing. The more a couple have been lifted up by their romantic attachment for each other, the more they can be hurt when the wearing out of its unreal element drops them to earth again. The ones who are stouthearted enough to count their own hurt a small matter, if they can still help the partner to have something to look forward to beyond the present difficulties, are matured by this part of their marriage experience, and later come to look back on what went before as a dreamlike time when they lived on nothing more substantial than hopes.

This is the testing period of the marriage. Each partner must continually get used to the new outline of the other's personality as it is showing itself, without losing sight of the value of the essential quality that persists. Of one thing both can be sure: each still has need of the other.

In today's mail comes a letter from a businessman who admits that he had got out of the habit of showing his wife how he felt about her in the rush and worry of trying to keep his head above water financially. Now that she in her loneliness has lost her heart to another man, the husband almost breaks into poetry in telling of his feelings. Not vindictive, he is just hopeless. If the wife could have had imagination enough to realize the strength of his need of her, she would never have wrapped herself in loneliness away from him.

The drop from the temporary bliss of the beginning of love to the lasting burden-sharing of the rest of life offers many a chance for hurt feelings. Those who lose confidence in their own or their partner's ability to keep on trying to live together on a reality basis are generally the ones who want to keep one foot in the dreamland of immaturity. If he drinks and she sulks, both would rather think themselves martyrs and talk over their troubles with sympathetic friends than get down to business and do something about their problems.

Quarrels are intense in proportion to the depth of tender emotion in the background. Not understanding what is happening to them, the husband and wife think it is the end of love, and he may be tempted to accept comfort from another woman, she from another man. Then they need desperately to know, "What is the case for monogamy?"

History shows that monogamy has always been accompanied by increasing vigor in the society or group practicing it, and that its opposite—freedom from social restraint in the relationships of men and women—has always been associated with social or group decay. But modern young people are interested in the meaning of monogamy for them personally.

Monogamy is a going on in the healthy spirit of meeting what life brings, not running away from it. Escape into a substitute relationship is a going back to the dreamlike stage of late adolescence, putting new promises ahead of present performance, and attempting to make life stand still, so that one may continue on the threshold of maturity without ever stepping over into the place where one must make good one's promises.

No human craving, from infancy to death, is stronger than that for security of affection. What misleads people into thinking of going outside their marriage association, or wanting to break it for a new one, is their failure to understand the slow growth of permanent affection. Looking back at the intensity of its beginning in romantic love, they suppose it is dwindling, when it is really taking root.

As a child that has been spoiled at home has a hard time getting used to the lesser attention he receives away from home, the married person who believes that courtship love is the essence of marriage finds it hard to come down to the quieter affection that can endure. This is the person who, unable to stand being valued only for his or her real worth, complains to an outsider, "Nobody understands me." The outsider, flattered, murmurs, "I do," and romanticizes about "this fine, unappreciated person," only to discover when it is too late that the person was only too well understood by the unfortunate first partner.

128

One may not be able to make oneself grow up suddenly and all at once, but one can hold on to the principles one knows to be worth fighting for, by the simple process of refusing to let go. All kinds of wonderful qualities needed in marriage may seem to be conspicuous in oneself chiefly by their absence, but one can always play for time. Even if infatuated with another person, one can hang on to what one knows is right until Time, the mighty leveler of passion, comes to one's help.

An exceptionally happy married woman, after going through this ordeal, said that at the time when she was almost carried away by an unexpected infatuation for a business associate of her husband's, it seemed as if nothing was real but the lover. Neither the memory of past happiness with the husband nor the thought of his future misery if she should leave him was able to mean more to her than so many words. Only, in her half-stupefied condition, she had the wit to remember, as one might recall the multiplication table without caring anything about it, that she had always previously despised people who acted on impulse without trying to find out the probable consequences. Therefore she stuck to her self-imposed rule that she would have no contact with the man, even by letter, until she could get over the strange numbness of her emotions toward her husband. Then, gradually but thoroughly, she came out of her trancelike infatuation, until she found it hard to remember that it had ever happened.

The time to put on the brakes in checking runaway emotions is before they gain momentum. While the feelings aroused still seem harmless, the person can redirect his or her energy toward a more desirable object such as finding new grounds of communion with the spouse or sublimating its expression by turning it into constructive artistic or social channels. To wait until disaster threatens before taking oneself in hand is to pile up, at best, a guilty feeling that one has not done one's best to meet the needs of the mate.

Those who "step out" in the frantic forties and foolish fifties complicate the picture for their younger observers. What they are trying to find is not so much a new thrill as the reliving of an old glow—the hopefulness of their lost youth. Not content to live over in memory the high hopes that were theirs when life was new—because of the gap between expectation and realization—they close their eyes to the new disillusionment they are heading for, and think only to shut out their sense of inadequacy in their present association by steering full steam ahead for another encounter, in which the odds are even more against them.

One may think one doesn't care much about the partner, one may get tired of listening to the same old jokes, the same set of worries, the same reminiscences; but let there be a misunderstanding, and one finds that one must care tremendously or one could not be so devastated. No association is so humdrum that it cannot be quickened into life, no matter how long it has been meagerly taking its course.

Certain types of people, whom we might lump together as a restless, discontented lot, enjoy "shopping around" for doctors, for jobs, for friends, for lovers, never staying long enough with any one doctor, job, friend, or lover to have to take any back talk. As soon as the first signs of a candid relationship appear, they are off, bag and baggage, to newer hunting grounds. We may suspect that what they really want is to outrun their own personality.

This appears in their willingness to slough off even their children, in an adolescent impatience with any barrier to an immediate desire. So contrary is this to nature that regret follows closely their decision. The children, however, are laden with a burden put on them by their parents. Instead of joyful confidence, they experience a divided affection. Driven to a choice of loyalties or caught between competing rivals who attempt to win their love, they are thereby denied security, the one gift every home owes a child.

Depending as he must upon his parents for this, it is a shattering experience for him to find that the twofold support of his existence is no longer holding together. He wants and needs not his mother or his father, nor just his mother and his father, but his two parents love-linked together as the one source of steadiness in a universe which otherwise is in flux and turmoil.

The child who finds his parents have given up trying to maintain their affectionate interdependence is hurt beyond any other hurt that can come to him. Precociously matured by being denied that security of encircling affection which is his right, he is forever cheated of his childhood and therefore can never become fully mature emotionally, but must have great gaps in what should have been the slow development of his emotions, before they hardened into adult form.

The monogamic fellowship normally encourages the coming of the child. Neither husband nor wife can awaken in the other the strong normal urges that come to expression in love fellowship, without bringing forth the desire that seems rooted in human nature for a child of their own. In any case, when the child does enter the home, experience soon makes plain his need of security. Where there is no monogamic commitment, he is forced into family life that is confused, incomplete, and uncertain. In such a situation, open as he is to first impressions, he suffers most, and not infrequently so deeply as to carry emotional scars for life. The friend of children recoils from the thought of any sort of transient motherhood or fatherhood. Monogamy provides a stable home in which each member—husband, wife and child—although they are copartners in love, has an indispensable, unique, and satisfying role.

Monogamy is not a fettering of human impulse, but a registration of the deepest yearnings of men and women. The laws that define and support it are merely man's efforts to express the common opinion that has taken form out of the experiences through the centuries of a great multitude of persons who, like ourselves, have sought success in marriage. Those who think of monogamy as something imposed on human nature through external authority, a sort of strait jacket of emotional restraint, are obtuse to the overwhelming testimony of human nature. Monogamy is not established by a thundering edict from Mount Sinai, but by the quiet, persistent inward-speaking of human need. The one-man-one-woman craving is so deeply laid in the structure of all of us that any other way of mating and establishing a home is alien to desire, the thought never arises, except when the one-time expectations have been lost through personality failure.

Monogamy is not something that suddenly and finally takes shape, a petrifying of emotion that for a season in courtship flourishes. It gets its vitality through a growth process, continues with life, a spreading of an affection always forward-looking; anything else is an indication of a faltering marriage. In the beginning love announces the awakening of mutual need. Then the feelings flow swift and strong and carry each toward the other. The impulse to possess, to annex, to have possession of the beloved, is a consuming hunger. It is a covetous grasping, a recognition that the other is indispensable. Out of this comes a union, and from then on, the two grow not only together, but also their common fellowship grows, becoming their way of life.

The passion to possess the other one, who seems external, fades away, and in its place comes the joy of mutual sharing, the security of an exploring fellowship. It is thus that monogamy offers love its fulfillment. There must be this welding of self with self if the emotionally awakened man or woman is to escape loneliness. Self-expansion in power, distinction, or pleasure does not suffice. Any by-oneself fulfillment only brings home the profounder need of a different achievement, not in separation, but through union, the fusion of two persons in a constant intimacy.

This growing together comes from no deliberate, effort-making program. It grows out of the affectionate living together. It is a day-by-day consolidation, not only of interest or experience, but of satisfactions. It is this that led Plato long ago to say that the man or woman apart from the other is incomplete, a partial person, hungering for the needed lover. Monogamy is, however, not a mere getting together; it is a growing together. It furnishes the opportunity for continued unrivaled intimacy, and its on-going not only strengthens the life together, but makes it pregnant with the forces that lead to character growth.

Monogamy is therefore a preference, usually so much a matter of course as to seem the natural way of living. This explains its supremacy among the schemes of human mating. It is a product of love ties, but only as these flourish in a maturing intimacy. It asks no more than that each member of the fellowship grow with the other.

Monogamy is indeed a test of character, but not in some extraordinary, aristocratic way that would put it out of the reach of most of us. Although its benefits cannot be had for the mere asking, it is denied to no one who in sincerity lives in love with the person of his choice. It is an achievement, but not in the sense that one eventually awakens to discover that he has at last arrived at a monogamic relationship. It is rather a hand-in-hand walking through life of a man and woman, each having chosen the other and offered his every possession. It as surely adds to character as it demands character.

The vitalizing union provides incentives that enrich both character and ambition. The two sharing a common life add more, do more, and feel more than each found possible in their one-time isolation. This in turn strengthens the union and makes each more indispensable to the other. They do not attempt to duplicate each other, but knowing that their love is secure, each gains through the life contact of the other. It was thus that Robert and Elizabeth Browning each affected the quality of the other's work, both being able to write deeper and more human poetry as a result of their marriage.

It is most important for an understanding of monogamy that it not be thought of as a monotony, a petering out of the energy of love until the high hopes of the confident lovers disappear in a drab, toilsome existence. This fading out does come to married people just as it does to those who have never married. Rightly used, however, monogamic fellowship protects by making adventure in life more zestful because it is shared. However hard and dreary experience becomes, it is more so if one walks alone and less so if its testing is met by two who travel onward in love. Monotony is always a reflection of inner losses. So long as we are alive to what is, so long as we have the feelings that uncover the zestfulness of things, we keep out of the desert. Monogamy cannot guarantee enthusiastic living, but undoubtedly, by encouraging mutual love, it protects the roots from which most of all each of us draws vitality.

When the relationship becomes monotonous, there is the same confession of failure as when day-by-day happenings grow stale and repellent. The difference is that when love goes, the fortress has been taken and all life flattens out.

The exclusiveness of monogamic fellowship, the out-coming of the deep hunger for a unique experience in affection, can be greatly misinterpreted by failing to see that it is human nature's effort to keep to the golden mean as one is driven by tremendous impulses toward the supreme man-woman comradeship. In all such relationships there is on one side the extreme which shows itself when one member of the intimacy crushes and destroys the personality of the other. This eventually spoils the union by making it a conquest of one by the other. The opposite disaster appears when there is no fusion at all but merely an alliance of two independent, self-centered persons who come together in the spirit of temporary self-interest and refuse to develop a common life. Even when they maintain the letter of the monogamic code, they lose its spirit.

In contrast with these unfortunates, victims of will-to-power and self-centered passion, those in monogamic fellowship enlarge the life they share. One often notices, as did Hudson, the naturalist, in his description of the English shepherd's home, that husband and wife reach such understanding that they share feeling without recourse to words; and gather so much in common that as they travel through the years they do, indeed, seem to grow even to look like each other. They winter and summer together, and when time sends the children to their own adventures, we hear these life-tested lovers, hand in hand, saying:

"Grow old along with me! The best is yet to be, The last of life, for which the first was made."

www.ingramcontent.com/pod-product-compliance
Lightning Source LLC
Chambersburg PA
CBHW071408280526
45787CB00001B/481